# ENDORSEMENTS

Teresa Ward does a brilliant job in her comprehensive writing, *Gateway to Dreams*. Whether you find yourself as a novice or one who has interpreted dreams for years, her knowledge through study and experience, creates tools and opens doors to the continuing adventure. People as spiritual creatures, find themselves soul searching for answers to life's goals. As the Creator pours Himself out to His creation through the realms of the Spirit, people are intrigued with the voice from within, drawing them close. *Gateway to Dreams* is one of those blessings that help you to understand your purpose and fulfill your journey into other dimensions through the language and power of dreams. Thanks, Teresa, for your timely and timeless gift.

JOHN AND RUTH FILLER
Overseers, The Gateway International, Coeur d'Alene, Idaho
Thegatewayintl.org

I read *Gateway to Dreams* and immediately started putting it into practice—it was that helpful. Teresa Ward does a great job of keeping it simple, yet insightful, fun, and engaging. It's clear to me that Teresa's lifetime of dream experience needs to be passed on. She'll push the envelope of what you think is possible, all the while keeping the process safe and non-intimidating. Her fluid approach takes into account that people are different, and she gives each individual the freedom to find out what their dreams mean to them!

CHRISTOPHER PAUL CARTER
Author of *In the Palaces of Heaven* and *Caught Up in the Spirit*
Discovertheheavens.org

The first time I met Teresa Ward I was taken by her honesty, gentleness, courage, and sincerity. She was one of the sweetest and the most positive people I'd ever met.

We all have dreams, and it is always refreshing to see different dream interpretations. Many of my own paintings have been inspired by my vivid dreams and visions.

I believe by understanding more about dream dimensions, we can uncover the mysteries of this life and the unknown, and I believe many will find Teresa Ward's perception of the complexity of dreams helpful and rewarding.

AKIANE KRAMARIK
Artist, Author, Child Prodigy
Artakiane.com

To be honest, I had no idea the subject of dreams had so many facets till I saw Teresa Ward's book. She breaks the matter down into detail yet keeps the subject engaging, simple and easy to read. The Bible predicts an increase of dreams and visions occurring prior to the second coming of Jesus. I encourage you to read this book and pay attention to the dreams in your life. You have a calling and destiny to account for and cannot afford to miss what heaven communicates to you while you're asleep. I'm glad Teresa wrote this, and you'll be glad too when you read it.

DR. LANCE WALLNAU
Lance Learning Group
Lancewallnau.com

I have known Teresa Ward since 2005. She has been a team player on ministry trips and at conferences where she was responsible for equipping and training in the realm of dreams. During those events many lives have been impacted greatly...that to me is the primary endorsement of this book. Fruit. As I read through *Gateway to Dreams*, I recognized Teresa wants to disclose those things that often are ignored regarding supernatural communication through dreams. She touches on subjects that are very specific that create a learning model in the realm of dream interpretation. I have had many prophetic dreams through the years and often have required the help of tools and Biblical understanding to process the dreams. In this book, Teresa makes the "Ancient Paths" simple. If you dream, and we all do...this book will bless you and mature you in your ability and insightful understanding of your own dreams, but also help you encourage others through their dreams. The realm of dreams is not limited to Christians, and as a result we can assist a generation that doesn't know God by bringing language and value to the dreams they carry about their destiny in God! Thanks for this insightful work!

DANNY STEYNE
Mountain of Worship
Themountain.org

# GATEWAY
## TO
# DREAMS

# GATEWAY TO DREAMS

## *3 Simple Steps to Dream Interpretation*

## TERESA WARD

DESTINY IMAGE® PUBLISHERS, INC.
P.O. Box 310, Shippensburg, PA 17257-0310
*"Promoting Inspired Lives."*

This book and all other Destiny Image and Destiny Image Fiction books are available at Christian bookstores and distributors worldwide.

Cover design by Dolores DeVelde,
http://fineartamerica.com/profiles/dolores-develde.html

For more information on foreign distributors, call 717-532-3040.
Reach us on the Internet: www.destinyimage.com.

ISBN 13 TP: 978-0-7684-0729-7
ISBN 13 eBook: 978-0-7684-0730-3

For Worldwide Distribution, Printed in the U.S.A.
1 2 3 4 5 6 7 8 / 19 18 17 16 15

# DEDICATION

I dedicate my first book to my heavenly Father God who infused me with *His* dreams from a very young age and kept me in the palm of His hand to make sure I would reach my destiny. Thank You, Father God, for choosing me to be Your child and for making my dreams come true. *You* are my shield and my exceedingly great reward. I'm truly blessed and highly favored!

I dedicate it to You, Jesus, my sweet and holy Savior; my brother who sticks closer than a friend; my perfect husband who is faithful, always protects me and never abandons or rejects me; my best friend who always listens, cares, and always believes in me; and my redeemer who is turning all things together for my good, redeeming the time and giving me a reward that goes Above & Beyond all I could ask or imagine!

I dedicate it to You, Holy Spirit, my precious helper and comforter. You are the one who leads me in the way I should go and the one who gently whispers wisdom to my heart and comfort to my soul. I could not begin or end each day without You.

I commit this book into Your hands, Father God, and ask You to bless all those who read it. May they discover hidden treasures in their dreams (Your sweet voice *is* the treasure), and may they know the depths of Your love for them. May Your loving kindness and unsearchable grace set them free to pursue their destiny in Christ Jesus!

*Commit your way to the Lord,*
*Trust also in Him,*
*And He shall bring it to pass* (Psalm 37:5).

At last…my dreams of this book have come to pass.

*For the vision is yet for an appointed time;*
*But at the end it will speak, and it will not lie.*
*Though it tarries, wait for it;*
*Because it will surely come,*
*It will not tarry* (Habakkuk 2:3).

# IN HONOR OF
# JOHN PAUL JACKSON

*John Paul Jackson went to be with the
Lord on February 18, 2015.*

John Paul,

If God would allow me to speak to you
This is what I would say;
How could I ever thank you
For where I am today?

I had a dream once about you (actually, many!)
And God revealed your worth;
You were an original Stradavarius,
And from you I was birthed.

You even prophecied that I would write...
This book and many more;
That I would be incredibly successful,
From all God had in store.

You opened my seer eyes,
And gave me an insatiable hunger;
To the realm of the supernatural,
To God's AWE and WONDER.

You taught me about God's justice,
You taught me about God's love;
You taught me about dreams and visions,
And humility that comes from above.

Your teaching gave me hope,
It inspired me to go higher;
It helped me through my darkest year,
It pulled me from the mire.

I pray I can impart,
All the gifts and the treasure;
You gave us to give to others,
Without fault, without measure...

You will forever be remembered, honored and cherished in my heart and in my walk with God. Thank you for sharing what God gave you with the rest of us. May we faithfully take the baton and go forward. May God credit your account for all the deposits you've made in each one of us. My heart is filled with much sorrow that you're gone and also an extravagant amount of gratitude for the privilege of having been personally taught by you.

# EXPRESSIONS OF GRATITUDE

First and foremost, I thank my Lord and Savior, Jesus Christ, for His amazing sacrifice on the cross so I could live for Him. I'm nothing without You. I thank my sweet and precious Father God for giving me the gift of dreaming and the love to share it with others so they may also know how much You love them and long to communicate with them. I thank the Holy Spirit for refreshing me daily and leading me in the way I should go. Thank You for helping me to help others and show the compassion You desire me to.

I thank all of my amazing parents: Gloria and Toney Hughey and Bob and Mary Lord for all the sacrifices they've made for me and all the love and support they've lavished on me to help me become who I am today. I thank God for each one of you. I'm truly blessed beyond measure! I pray God continues to make all *your* dreams come true!

I thank my two remarkable sons, Brandon and Logan. You both have taught me so much about myself, and your beautiful and generous hearts have revealed God to me. May God guide you and guard you all the days of your life, and may all your God-given dreams come true!

Enormous thanks to my publisher, Destiny Image, especially Ronda Ronalli, Mykela Krieg, John Martin, and the sales team, for believing in me and sincerely caring above and beyond the call of duty. You are all amazing and I'm incredibly humbled and grateful for the love and support I've received.

Thanks to Roland and Anna Ludlam. Roland, thank you for your countless and painstaking hours of meticulous work for Above & Beyond. You continue to turn my abstract thoughts into tangible ideas wrapped in beautiful packages! Anna, you are the epitome of love and grace, and you are better than a best friend! I thank you both for being faithful and true friends who endure when most quit. Your prayers, wisdom, and graciousness are rare and precious gems and you both have taught me so much. Thanks for living and loving Above & Beyond!

I thank Dolores DeVelde for her amazing talent in creating the artwork for this book. You are truly anointed, and I pray this is just the beginning of a life-long friendship that glorifies God. May you be blessed in all you do and may people encounter the majesty of the living God when they experience your artwork.

I extend my deepest and heartfelt thanks to Bill Ruttan, Jennifer Stapleton, Jim Van Law, Julie Woellert, Lily Herndon-Weaks, and Paul Bolte…. Each of you know why and words cannot express the depths of my gratitude.

Last, but definitely not least, I want to express gratitude to all who have supported me, poured into my life over the years, and encouraged me through all the pain—wow, it's been a long journey. Thanks to all who gave selflessly in prayer, financially, and with the sacrifice of your time. Though all your names are not specifically listed here because the pages could not contain you all, you are held dear to my heart and I keep you lifted before God in my prayers.

May God richly bless all who continually bless and support Above & Beyond, myself, and my two sons. I'm deeply moved by your faithfulness and I ask God to pour back to you a blessing so big you cannot contain it!

In loving memory of dear friends and family who departed in 2014. We look forward to seeing you again in Heaven!

Christine Potts—my dear cousin and friend. I will miss your spark, spunk, smile, and laughter.

Hannah Strickland—you are truly unforgettable! We can hear you singing in the great cloud of witnesses!

Al Andersen—a generous man who was all heart.

# CONTENTS

## Section 1

# BUCKLE UP AND PREPARE FOR YOUR DREAM ADVENTURE!

*Chapter 1*

# ENTERING THE GATEWAY
# TO YOUR DREAMS

## FIRST STOP: THE DREAM CAFÉ

Hello, and welcome! This book will serve you as a *dream café* of sorts. It will be your gateway to dreams, visions, and a biblical perspective of the ways God communicates with you. I've confirmed your divine appointment, and you are cordially invited to participate in an interactive experience that will propel you into your spiritual destiny. I encourage you to aspire higher and *reach for God in a fresh, new, and exciting way!*

My name is Teresa and I will be your server today. If you are spiritually thirsty, perhaps instead of a latte or java, you'll allow me to serve you our specialty—*a lotta* Jehovah (God). He will cause your cup to run over, and we give free eternal refills.

To satisfy your spiritual hunger, our chef has prepared a generous helping of hope, drizzled with destiny. Discover the recipe to your dream life with our Ancient Mystic Model of dream interpretation found in the Bible.

Indulge your spiritual senses and delve into our "dreamy" desserts, which include how to understand and interpret dream symbols, how to journal your dreams, and how to discover the voice of God in your everyday life. Or perhaps you would prefer for us to whip you up a sweet dream interpretation with two scoops of insight.

Now sit back, relax, and allow God to illuminate your heart and give you understanding of how He may be speaking to you personally.

Let your dream journey begin!

## WHAT THIS BOOK IS

In order to save you time as you look over the table of contents, or "the menu," let me explain what this book is and is not.

This book serves as a simple quick-start guide to understanding your dreams. It is my privilege to share with you my personal experience with dreams and how it propelled me into incredible intimacy with God. My goal is to give you the tools you need to interpret *any* symbol and compile your own symbol dictionary to use for your dreams, visions, and natural and spiritual experiences.

It may challenge you, it may excite you, it may propel you into your own intimate encounter with God, or it may even offend you. I heard someone once say that at times God may offend the mind to reveal the heart. I was also a skeptic once, so I understand those who have reservations, and I would even agree that it is wise to have reservations.

## WHAT THIS BOOK IS NOT

This book is *not* a comprehensive, in-depth biblical study of dreams, interpretation, or the voice of God. This book is also not a dream dictionary. It is not a debate and it is not the answer to everything concerning dreams. It is also not a formula for dream interpretation or for hearing God. Dreams, interpretation, and God's voice are very deep topics that cannot be covered in one book.

I believe the instructions I received from God about what to include were to give you a very simple and quick beginning so you would have hope and a desire to study deeper.

For now, I simply encourage you to take a step of faith knowing there is so much more than what is inside this book. Don't simply take my word for things—pray and ask God about everything and study ancient Scripture.

If you desire to know more after this book, I offer Dream Workshops, Dreaminars®, Dreamcasts®, Dreamology® courses, a Dreamscapes® phone and tablet app, and I will also be writing more books. You can find information on how to connect with me and my ministry, Above & Beyond, on the back pages of this book.

## THE DREAM DARE: WHO THIS BOOK IS FOR

Okay, so where do we start? There are several types of people who are holding this book in their hands.

First, there may be many who may think dreams are just pizza and bad burritos talking.

Others of you believe dreams have psychological meaning, but may not believe God can or still does use dreams to speak to people today.

Some of you may not even believe in God at all.

Yet some of you believe God still speaks in dreams, but you may not know how to understand them. You also may not realize that the principless of how He speaks in dreams can be applied to your everyday life.

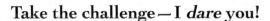

## Take the challenge—I *dare* you!

## WHICH DARE IS FOR YOU?

### 1. *The dare for those who don't believe in God or that dreams can come from Him:*

For those of you who don't have a relationship with God or don't believe in Jesus Christ as God's one and only Son and the Savior, you will be apprehensive to give this model of interpretation a try because it's "too religious" and comes from the ancient Hebraic, Aramaic, and Greek scrolls—a source we call the Bible—and you may not be familiar with it, comfortable with it, or agree with it. Your inclination will be to blow the entire thing off because you've never encountered God or believe He wants to encounter you in this way.

I encourage you to delve into the depths of hidden mystic revelations God has buried—rewards waiting to be discovered and unveiled. You will have an advantage even over many Christians who don't search the ancient scrolls with excitement or expectation of finding hidden mysteries. There were ancient mystics all through the Bible who have shared incredible and eternal insights that only a non-religious mind will be able to take hold of and comprehend.

Sometimes, it's so simple we don't see it because we're looking for the complicated or the religious. I invite you to try the Ancient Mystic Model of dream and symbolic interpretation that comes from God. What have you got to lose? You might discover a loving God who has been pursuing you your entire life! *I dare you to just try it for 30 days.*

## 2. The dare for those who believe in God, but not dream interpretation (It's all pizza and burritos, right?):

Then there are those who love God, have a relationship with Him, but the relationship is defined by your terms and you tend to be stuck in religious bondage, putting God in a tiny box you don't allow Him to come out of. Even the term *mystic* bothers you, and you think it's a new age or demonic term. However, *mystic* can simply mean to have divine understanding, and who better to have divine understanding than God and His people? You tend to get hung up on the way something is worded over the application of spiritual revelation.

For you, this book will not be "religious" enough. It will be difficult for you to comprehend that God uses spiritual principles as well as Scripture, and that He is actually very funny at times and incredibly clever. You will want everything to be in the Bible, when in fact everything is not in the Bible. The Bible even says in John 21:25, "And there are also many other things that Jesus did, which if they were written one by one, I suppose that even the world itself could not contain the books that would be written. Amen."

Cars and cell phones were not in the Bible. That doesn't mean God can't use them in our dreams or in life to speak to us. Gravity is not in Scripture, but it doesn't mean it doesn't exist. I can believe all day long that gravity doesn't exist because it's not in Scripture, but if I jump off a roof, I will fall to the ground because of gravity.

Everything God does and says, however, will always align with the Word of God, the principles of God, and the nature of God. I find it so amazing that Christians can believe that Jesus loves them so much that He went to the cross and suffered an excruciating death for them, but they aren't willing to believe that He loves them so much He would choose to speak to them in a simple dream that He, Himself, created. Is there any length God will not go to love us? Isn't God the Creator?

Even if you don't believe dreams have meaning, isn't God the one who created us to dream? God does nothing without purpose, and if He created us to dream, dreams must have purpose and significance.

God promises that if you seek Him, you will find Him. He also says in Matthew 7:9, "Or what man is there among you who, if his son asks for bread, will give him a stone?" Again, in Luke 11:11-13:

> *If a son asks for bread from any father among you, will he give him a stone? Or if he asks for a fish, will he give him a serpent instead of a fish? Or if he asks for an egg, will he offer him a scorpion? If you then, being evil, know how to give good gifts to your children, how much more will your heavenly Father give the Holy Spirit to those who ask Him!*

Just because our soul—which is the mind, will, and emotions—processes its own dreams, or the enemy perverts the original thing God created and influences some dreams, that doesn't mean God stops using dreams to speak to us. He is the same yesterday, today, and forever.

*We dare you to simply ask God if He's speaking to you in your dreams* and be willing to hear an answer that may not agree with your assumptions. Apply the principles laid out in this book, open your heart, and you just might hear God in a fresh new way!

## 3. *The dare for those who simply believe in God and dream interpretation:*

This is for those of you who simply believe God speaks this way and you desire a deeper level of intimacy with Him. That's who this book was really written for—not the unbeliever or the Christian, necessarily, but for all those who are simply looking for God and want to understand how He may be speaking to them. It is a journey to discover spiritual intimacy with our amazing and beloved Creator who longs for an intimate relationship with each and every one of us.

This book was written because God told me to write it for people who needed hope and for those who believed there was more. He loves you with depths of love you cannot comprehend, and He's excited you are looking for Him! He promises that if you look for Him, you will find Him. He wants to fill you with hope, encouragement, love, and destiny. For you, just proceed with an open heart filled with expectation! *We dare you to dive deeper!*

## FROM DREAM SKEPTIC TO DREAM SCHOLAR

I understand if you're skeptical! I was a skeptic until God got my attention and began speaking directly to me in my dreams and telling me how to interpret them. When I began interpreting dreams the way He directed, my dreams began to make sense and often everything fell into place or happened just as I interpreted it.

The challenge is to just try. What He did for me He will do for you. Let God out of a box and just see if He speaks to you in this way. What do you have to lose? Even the dreams that are a reflection of our emotions have valuable insight. What if it's not pizza and burritos? What if the Creator of the universe, the Creator of your very soul, is longing to communicate with you and is trying to get your attention? What if He has answers for you or inventions or warnings? What if He desires to bring you healing, hope and encouragement, or wisdom and direction?

My goal is to simply help you to begin thinking metaphorically and symbolically so you can hear God all the time. He has communicated this way since the beginning of time, and I personally believe it is His preferred way to speak because it requires us to apply our heart to gain understanding, which, in essence, is wisdom.

*Wisdom is the principal thing; therefore get wisdom. And in all your getting, **get understanding** (Proverbs 4:7).*

*How much better to get wisdom than gold! And to **get understanding** is to be chosen rather than silver (Proverbs 16:16).*

It's okay to feel both open-minded and skeptical. Just ask God for wisdom as you enter your own dream journey. God is the ultimate Dream Weaver. A dream from God is treasure longing to be discovered, wisdom and understanding waiting to be found. I am confident if you just ask God to reveal Himself this way, He will be faithful to show you He's been waiting for you!

**A dream from God is treasure longing to be discovered, wisdom and understanding waiting to be found.**

*Chapter 2*

# WHAT MAKES THIS BOOK DIFFERENT?

## APPLICATION VS. THEORY: THE DIVINE DIVING BOARD (JUMP IN, THE WATER IS GREAT!)

One thing that sets this book apart is that it's not just about the theory and theology of dream interpretation. The best way to learn is just to jump in and get started, and that's what I intend to help you do! I'm convinced if you have immediate success, you will want to then apply yourself to understand the deeper, more complex things concerning dream interpretation, and your desire to learn will propel you into deeper levels of intimacy with God.

In the same way that people approach going to the pool for a swim, some are hesitant at first, afraid the water is too cold or that they may get in way over their head and not be able to swim. If that's you, your approach will be to cautiously proceed and allow yourself to get used to the water—or, in this case, the ideas presented here.

Others of you love adventure and just jump in the water no matter what the temperature may be, and you will be the ones who immediately apply the suggestions to see if they work for you.

No matter what your approach or hesitations are, don't sit this one out—*jump in! The water is great and you will have fun!* That old myth about staying out of the water for 30 minutes after you eat kept all of us from having 30 more minutes of fun!

I have included important summary points at the conclusion of many chapter, titled "Jedi Dream Tips." I hope to provoke a smile and a memory of the famous *Star Wars* movies—the Jedi being those dedicated to spiritual wisdom. May the Force (who is God's Holy Spirit) be with you!

## PURSUING THE ANCIENT PATH: MODEL, NOT METHOD!

Now that you've decided to take the Dream Dare, it's important to point out I'm sharing with you an Ancient Mystic Model of interpretation found in the Hebrew, Aramaic, and Greek scrolls of the Bible, and I do *not* endorse a method.

The difference between a model and a method is that a model is a standard or example. Method implies a systematic way of doing something or a specific technique or procedure to be used the same way every time. You can think of a method as more of a formula. The problem with using a formula for interpreting dreams is that God is *not* a formula or method you can duplicate exactly the same way every time. He is a person and He desires to be pursued just as we do. He is a personal God who speaks very individually to people; what may be effective for one may not work for another.

Formulas indicate something can be duplicated over and over exactly the same way each time, which is simply not true for developing a relationship with God. We don't treat our own children exactly the same way, and neither does God. Formulas are often found in witchcraft, spells, evil incantations, etc., and these things are detestable to God. He plainly says He hates them! (See Deuteronomy 18:10-12.)

Ultimately, I believe the main issue is that the use of formulas removes the need for God. If you can do it on your own through a formula, why would you need God? It's the age-old struggle of pride and power or humility and surrender. God requires humility to enter into His presence. He will also not allow you to package Him in a nice, neat package you can sell for profit. There's a story in the Bible of Jesus turning over the tables of the money changers you may want to read up on! (See Matthew 21:12-16.)

Many times the meaning of a dream almost ends up insignificant or irrelevant compared to the act of the pursuit of God in the process. The search is about developing your relationship with God and spending time with Him.

God speaks in a myriad of ways we are still discovering. All of creation speaks of God, and we will not have an excuse or be able to say we didn't know there was a God and that He was speaking. It says in the ancient Greek in the biblical book of Romans, "For since the creation of the world His invisible attributes are clearly seen, being understood by the things that are made, even His eternal power and Godhead, so that they [men/women] are without excuse" (Romans 1:20). That verse basically says that everything visible speaks of God, even though He is invisible, and God can and does speak in everything.

I believe dreams are just one of a multitude of ways God speaks to people. I also believe God is the only correct interpreter of dreams, visions, trances, and natural circumstances. In the Hebraic scrolls of Genesis, there was a dream interpreter named Joseph. He was a godly man and was asked to interpret a dream. Genesis 40:8 says, "And they said to him, 'We each have had a dream, and there is no interpreter of it.' So Joseph said to them, 'Do not interpretations belong to God? Tell them to me, please.'" This verse reveals that God is the only correct dream interpreter, and we need Him to understand them.

While not all dreams are from God—in fact, very few are—God is still the one who created us with the ability to dream, so I believe they still have purpose. God does nothing without purpose, and learning to interpret will help you discover the treasures God has strategically hidden just for you!

Learning how God speaks metaphorically will significantly propel your ability to hear Him speaking to you every day in every way. God uses things you understand to explain things you don't understand. That's how He has always communicated—it's His nature. There are more than 8,000 figures of speech and metaphorical references in the ancient scrolls of the Bible.

## DISCOVERING HIDDEN TREASURES ALONG THE ANCIENT PATH

God has amazing hidden treasures waiting to be found along His ancient path. When following the path to correct dream interpretation found in the Bible, we must consider approaching it in the same way we approach His voice throughout the Holy Scriptures.

In Scripture, the *ancient way* means the everlasting, eternal, or perpetual (forever) way. God is the Ancient One. He created wisdom before He created us. If we ask of Him for the ancient or wise way, the way that will be eternally and forever the correct way, He will lead us on the correct path to understand. God desires that we understand, and He longs to bless us with wisdom and lead us in the right way that will benefit us. The key is that our hearts must *want* to know the right way. My years of diligent study have brought me to believe God chooses symbolic ways of communication so that we must meditate and also apply our heart to gain understanding. We must *want* to understand.

The difference between interpreting Scripture and interpreting dreams, however, is that when interpreting Scripture it's imperative to approach it very *objectively*, whereas dreams must be interpreted very *subjectively*. Let's take a quick look at the difference.

## Objectivity

To be *objective* means to be based on facts and not influenced by feelings, etc. When you interpret Scripture, you must first begin by observing the text, then interpreting the text in the context in which it was written, and lastly applying it to your life. When interpreting Scripture, it's vitally important to allow Scripture to interpret Scripture. To do that means to look for other similar examples to see what God has already said about a specific thing in other places throughout the Bible, because God's nature never changes and context is everything. When interpreting Scripture, we have to be very careful not to add to or subtract from what is there, because that would change the meaning of what God intended as He spoke through various people by inspiration of the Holy Spirit.

## Subjectivity

Dreams, however, are very *subjective* and are often based on personal feelings, experiences, opinions, etc. Subjectivity is individualistic and changes depending on the person, situation, and various other factors. Dreams are very personal and deal with the dreamer's own experiences, emotions, knowledge, etc. We must be careful to approach dream interpretation subjectively and allow not only for personal interpretation for each dreamer, but also each individual dream.

As you step onto the ancient path of biblical dream interpretation—the Ancient Mystic Model—be careful with each dream, each symbol, each question you have concerning them. First ask God for understanding before you consult *any* other resources. Then search the ancient Scriptures to find examples God may have already used to explain something to us. We can easily and unintentionally get into the habit of hearing someone say a particular symbol means something specific and forget to ask God what it means first, then what it may represent to our specific situation, and more importantly why it means what it does. The "why" is very often more important than the "what."

With dreams, I have said and will continue to say a million times, just as in Scripture, *"Context is the key to correct interpretation!"*

## USING A BIBLICAL ANCIENT MYSTIC MODEL

There are many methods of dream interpretation circulating, such as Freudian, Jungian, or Gestalt's to name a few. As I've already mentioned, I use and teach an Ancient Mystic Model of dream interpretation (model not method!) found in Holy Scripture. I believe the Lover of our soul, the one who created us and our destiny, also created the only correct model of dream interpretation. God has been speaking in dreams since the beginning of humankind. He continues to speak in dreams to us, longing for our hearts to respond to His promptings and invitations. He desires an intimate and supernatural relationship with every single person.

I have accessed ancient scrolls and researched how God spoke in dreams and how He has spoken symbolically for all of eternity. I have specifically researched how dream mystics, including Daniel and Joseph in the ancient Hebraic scrolls, discovered the hidden mysteries of how to interpret dreams correctly and understand what God was saying in them.

Other methods of dream interpretation come from a psychological point of view and deal with dreams from a perspective that they are always internally created by your psyche. Most believe dreams are always about the dreamer. They think dreams are meant to simply deal with emotions and aid in self-change. While I believe that many dreams are given for those *exact* purposes, I also have a perspective that allows for dreams to come externally from

God, and I will unveil for you the supernatural side of dreams, which includes God in the equation. The word *psyche* comes from the Greek word that means "soul." I will show you how I also include the spirit in our interpretations, not just the body or the soul, which is the mind, will and emotions. We are made up of three parts—body, soul, and spirit. I will show you how dreams can come from all three—not just the soul or psyche.

Believing that dreams are always internally created will not allow dreams to come from God Himself or allow for eternal and spiritual change. Nor does this belief allow for dreams about things we have no knowledge of—what some refer to as prophetic dreams. Many inventions are given in dreams about things of which the dreamer had no previous knowledge.

Other methods of interpretation believe dreams have only one meaning. However, ancient Scripture teaches that there is the ability to have a supernatural level to dreams. Just as Scripture can and does have multiple meanings, so can dreams if they are from God! When God speaks, there is no measuring the depths of the hidden knowledge in what He says.

**There is no measuring the depths of hidden knowledge in what God says to you.**

The main thing to consider if you use other methods of dream interpretation is that if you exclude God from the equation, then you will never come up with the same interpretation God does for the dreams in ancient Scripture. The reason is because the other methods have removed the spiritual element and you cannot hear from God without the Spirit of God. If the interpretation method does not come *from* God, it will not lead you *to* God.

I challenge you to try this model of interpretation. I believe as you experience true spiritual encounters in your dreams, you will discover the once hidden voice of God to now be revealed in everything all the time. I believe you will discover the treasures hidden in your sleep, and you will be infused with hope and find a new level of intimacy with your heavenly Father God.

While the strategies I share will hopefully invite you into a successful experience of hearing from God, ultimately God will only reveal certain secrets to those who serve Him and carry His Spirit inside of them. Once again, *only the Spirit of God knows the mind of God*. If you do not have His Spirit, you will often find it difficult to know or understand what He is saying. If you're not sure if you have His Spirit, or if you would like to invite the light of God to dwell in your inner being and receive the fullness of His Spirit, see Chapter 10, "The Secret Gateway: Invite the Light." There, you will be introduced to the light and love of God, which will send you on the pathway toward your spiritual destiny.

## Sweet and Simple

One of the major things that make this book different is that it is intended to be a fun, interactive kick-start approach to discovering God's voice for yourself! Dream interpretation can become very overwhelming at times, and you probably already know that if you're reading this! I want you to begin your dream adventure *today* with practical steps to get you up and running as fast as possible so you are encouraged to continue investigating.

As you continue to navigate your way through the pages in this book, which will be a fun spiritual scavenger hunt of sorts, please keep in mind this book is only a brief introduction to the realm of dream interpretation and there is still an extravagant amount of treasure to hunt for beyond these pages.

## THE GUITAR LESSON: LEARNING TO KEEP IT FUN!

It is typical and understandable when a subject is being taught that there are procedures and foundations that need to be laid and taught first before moving on. When it comes to spiritual issues, though, we have to be careful not to live by "the law." This happens over and over in spiritual circles without our even realizing it. Dream interpretation is not a step-by-step procedure, but one that is a unique spiritual symphony that God orchestrates. Correct dream interpretation is totally dependent upon God's Word, His nature, and most importantly His Holy Spirit, who is the one who gives the correct interpretation.

As I began to write this book and teach others everything God was unfolding to me, I wondered how to best convey God's wisdom for a strong foundation. Then God reminded me of the guitar lesson! I took guitar lessons when I was in fourth grade. Back then, I had to learn all the basics and foundational principles first. (Sound familiar?) First I was taught about the guitar itself, how to read music, and then to play only one note at a time. Not only did every song seem to sound the same playing one note at a time, but the songs I had to play were less than motivational—"Old McDonald," "Jingle Bells," and "Hot Cross Buns." I wasn't playing anything that was on the radio or any songs to motivate me to keep learning. I was so discouraged thinking it would take years before I could play "real music" that was on the radio. I was not allowed to learn chords until I perfected every single note. Practicing notes was *no* fun, and I had no desire to continue.

When my youngest son wanted to take guitar lessons, I searched for a dynamic teacher so he wouldn't be discouraged like I was. I found a fun, young guitar teacher for my son, and he was also a worship leader for a local church in the area. I will never forget the first lesson! I watched as the teacher quickly taught my son about the guitar as he had my son hold it. He gave him written instructions to memorize later at home. The teacher pointed out the strings' names, the frets, and how to strum up and down. Within ten minutes, the teacher showed my son where to put each finger to create a chord. *Yes! A chord in the first lesson!* He went on to show him how to strum while holding the chord. Then he showed him another chord and how to transition between chords.

By the time we left the first 30-minute lesson (yes, you read that right—only 30 minutes!), the teacher had taught my son four or five chords and he could play the song "Live Like You Were Dying" by Tim McGraw—a song my son loved. You can't imagine how excited my son was leaving the first lesson knowing how to play a popular song that was on the radio! He felt like a rock star and was so excited that he could play the guitar. Every week after each lesson, he played more and more songs immediately. As weeks went on, the teacher would infuse the foundational elements of music into each lesson. My son would come home and practice with excitement! He *wanted* to learn the foundational elements because he had first learned to love the music itself and was given the encouragement immediately that he could do it!

When inquiring of God how to approach teaching dream interpretation, I felt God told me to do the same thing! What I feel He instructed me to do was to teach you "interpretation chords" first, so you will discover how you can interpret and then you will want to continue to study deeper. If encouraged quickly, you will be more likely to pursue God's voice, knowing God *wants* you to understand, and you will be excited about what He is saying. I pray this is true for you.

## GOD IS FUN!

Wow! What if we approached people and showed them the loving and fun side of God first, just like the fun guitar lesson? They would fall so madly in love with Him that they would be encouraged to get to know Him deeper, and they would *want* to learn about His ways. Instead, we give people a list of all the things they can't do and warnings of the wrath of God if they do, so they think God is a mean old man who is always angry and they'll never please Him. So why try? In reality, God longs for people to have fun with Him and experience His love. When we love someone, we want to please the person. Let's focus on God's love and let Him reveal Himself to people instead of insisting that people follow our religious rules to find Him.

Thinking things have to be done a certain way and only one way is religious thinking. God wants out of the box we've put Him in. He is able to show Himself in ways we have not even thought of yet. We think God has to agree with our way of thinking instead of asking Him if there's a way we haven't thought of.

Jesus did not lay a foundation of teaching before He loved people who did not know Him. He loved them first, met their needs, and then they desired to know Him more! He would heal people and *then* tell them to sin no more. He didn't say, "First go to Bible school and get a degree, then do everything perfectly, and then I will consider healing you if I feel you've learned all you're supposed to know." We need to find new ways to teach. We need to meet the desire of the heart and ignite the passion in people first—then they will want to know more. I'm in no way speaking of compromise. Let me be clear that I am not implying we try methods that contradict God's nature or His Word.

## YOUR DIVINE APPOINTMENT

Are you ready for your "dream guitar lesson"? I dare you to delve into the depths of true spiritual intimacy that will propel you into your destiny and help you discover why you were created. You will embark on a journey that will take you into the very heart of God. It is my prayer that this book will ignite a fire within that will empower you to aspire higher. This is a divine appointment for you to encounter God. If you take the challenge, you will never be the same.

## JEDI DREAM TIPS:

- God uses things you understand to explain the things you don't.

- Few dreams are actually from God.

- There are over 8,000 figures of speech in Scripture.

- Dreams are to be interpreted subjectively.

- Dreams can have multiple meanings.

- If an interpretation doesn't come *from* God, it will not lead you *to* God.

# Chapter 3

# SWEET DREAMS

## PRELUDE TO AN ADVENTURE

A warm breeze gently embraced me while the summer sun kissed my face as I played in the yard beside my home in St. Charles, Illinois. Constantly contending with flashes of *déjà vu* and recalling dreams I had while playing outside, images and voices would appear in my mind as though they were commercials trying to get my attention. Little did I know then that it was God longing for me to take notice, using dreams and visions of the night to captivate me. He had been speaking to me that way my entire life, and I never pursued His voice until years later.

I was always curious why I constantly remembered my dreams from my childhood and up until about 2002. I wondered why they would continually flash before me. I would dream all night, every night and many times would even get up in the middle of the night, go back to bed, and pick up the dream where I left off. I could then go back to sleep the next night and begin the same dream again and carry on for several days in a row. It was like a mini-series that I would return to each night to tune into another dream episode.

Beyond the age of about five, adults bombard children with comments like, "Grow up," "Quit imagining things," "Don't let your imagination run away with you," and "That's just your imagination." We begin to slowly but methodically devalue the imaginations God gave us. Imagination is where creativity happens. Where would we be without those who have allowed their imaginations to run away and explore an infinite measure of possibilities? God gave us our internal movie screen called the imagination. Can God be limited to the confines of something that is not allowed to be big? He is a vast and big God and can only fit inside of an imagination that allows Him to be infinite. Our imaginations are the internal screens that God plays His love for us on. Some of us don't feel God's love because we simply cannot "imagine" that He would love us so much. To have faith is to be able to *imagine* how much God can do.

Many athletes accomplish their personal goals by first imagining or seeing themselves achieving them. Salespeople are encouraged to see or imagine the entire process happening before it happens in order to increase their skill and techniques. Why is our imagination so powerful in helping us accomplish goals? I had a dream once and heard the Lord say, "If you can see it, you can believe it." Belief is faith. Faith is what propels us to accomplish things. Our imagination is the blank screen and we decide what is played on it or who gets to play their movie on it. The key is to keep our imagination sanctified, or holy, and not allow unholy things to be played on it. We must also guard against not using it at all because that, in essence, is unbelief.

God has always spoken in diverse ways. The biblical scrolls reveal that God speaks in metaphors, riddles, dark speech, dreams, visions, trances, mysteries, hard sayings, allegories, acrostics, poetry, numbers, colors, enigmas, names, oracles, parables, idioms, shadows, types, circumstances, weather, and prophetic acts, just to begin to name a handful. His Word says in Romans 1:20 that all of creation speaks of Him and men will be without excuse and will not be able to say they didn't know about Him. He speaks in hidden ways on almost every page of every ancient letter or scroll. In the scroll of Isaiah 55:9, He Himself says, "For as the heavens are higher than the earth, so are My ways higher than your ways, and My thoughts than your thoughts."

There is no way we can understand God because He is infinite and all-knowing. We see and know very little. It is a comforting thing that God is so vast and infinite. I wouldn't want a God who knows only a little more than I do or a God who cannot see the entire picture from beginning to end. To reduce God to our way of thinking is reducing ourselves to ignorance. To think that a God who has created everything that exists thinks the way us finite humans think or understand is scary and ridiculous. I find relief that there is no way for me to know everything about God. I would not want such a small God.

> *"For My thoughts are not your thoughts, nor are your ways My ways," says the Lord. "For as the heavens are higher than the earth, so are My ways higher than your ways, and My thoughts than your thoughts"* (Isaiah 55:8-9).

The following pages of this book hold the account of how I personally learned that my dreams held meaning, and I will give you an account of how God has personally taught me things He wants me to share with you.

If you are skeptical of the model that is being used or of the approach I have learned to use, I challenge you to take a month's worth of dreams and put it to the test. I double dream dare you!

God is absolutely speaking to you, whether you realize it or believe it or not. He even knew you would read this book, and He can use it to speak to you specifically about your life, your heart, and possibly parts of your spiritual destiny. Learning how to decipher what God is saying in metaphors and symbolism will also escort you into a supernatural realm of hearing Him all the time in all of life. How we interpret dreams and visions can also be applied to the things that are happening in our life. If we will begin interpreting events and situations in our lives as we do in dreams and visions, we will discover loving messages, warnings, and wisdom that will contribute to the success of our life and launch us into our destiny. Learning to interpret will also help you deeper understand the pages of Scripture! You will begin to take more notice of the details you read and ask God, "Why this and not that?" or "Why that color or name or measurement?" You will begin to unearth hidden treasures on every page!

## THE ADVENTURE BEGINS

In the first part of 2002, I was flipping through TV channels desperately wanting something that would inspire me or lift my spirits. That time in my life was the most difficult time I had ever been through, and I was desperately grasping for things that would give me hope of destiny and purpose and pull me out of the severe depression I was in.

As the remote diligently searched for something to rescue me from the depression of the day, I heard a man talking about how God speaks in dreams and visions. I listened in amazement. I had been a prolific dreamer all my life and had always wondered why I was constantly reminded of my dreams, even dreams I had years prior. I'm not quite sure why I never searched out their meaning.

After listening to this man of God on television explain how God can speak in dreams and visions and watching him interpret the dreams of people in the audience, my heart was pounding with hope and curiosity. I had to know more. I immediately ordered an audio teaching set he offered and anxiously awaited its arrival.

The audio set finally came, and I listened to all six recordings and let the hope that perhaps God was speaking to me sink into my spirit. I eventually allowed the newness of the discovery to wear off, and I basically forgot most of what I had heard. One thing I remembered him saying was that it's important to write your dreams down. I periodically wrote some down and tucked them away to be forgotten about.

About six months had gone by, and suddenly I began to realize that some of the dreams I had written down six months prior were coming true. This both captivated me and scared me! God now had my full attention. These dreams were warning dreams, and this was no longer theory that dreams had meaning but proof to me personally that God was in control and He wanted to warn me of things to come in order to protect me. In His amazing love, He showed me, through my dreams, the plans the enemy of my soul, who is satan (I don't capitalize his name on purpose), had been devising in order to bring me even further than the depressed pit I was already in.

There was no more treating my dreams as a fun hobby as time allowed. No more thinking it was bad burritos or pizza. No more believing all dreams are created from within to simply help us to better ourselves, subconsciously deal with issues, or all the rest of the psychobabble that is floating around out there. Not that those things aren't also true sometimes, but in all the years I had been in church since I was a child, no one ever told me God still speaks in dreams! God was speaking directly to me, making some things unmistakably clear about things I could not have known.

After realizing God was warning me and speaking to me, curiosity, some holy fear, and an immeasurable amount of excitement leapt into my heart, and I was infused with hope again. The God of the universe loved me enough to communicate with me, to lead me to someone who would lead me to Him, and to open up my eyes and my heart to the destiny He had prepared in advance for me to discover and fulfill. The exciting thing about this is that because you are reading this book, this is part of His plan to get *your* attention about *your* dreams and destiny, too!

I once again, with passionate fervor this time, picked up the audio recordings and devoured them every day for weeks on end. I took meticulous notes and replayed them numerous times in hopes of catching some missed nuance that would lead me to deeper discovery. I poured my heart, soul, and mind into trying to understand my dreams. There was much (most) that was not covered in the teaching, and I quickly discovered that I had only enough information to make me dangerous with my interpretations. I knew some stuff now, but only enough to further confuse me because of what I didn't know.

The hunt for treasures in my dreams had begun, and the hunger would never be satisfied, even to this day. In my naïveté at the time, I thought that if I could simply take all the courses this person and their organization had to offer, I would be given all the answers, be given a dream dictionary with all the symbolism, and I would be able to interpret all my dreams. At this point I had not missed writing down any dreams that I could remember, and my questions about their meaning was increasing into a crescendo that would never end.

I immediately booked three courses back to back that were all to happen in a period of one solid week in two different states across the country. Normally people would take only one at a time and wait months or a year before taking another, but I was so hungry and desperate to find answers that I dove into the depths as fast as I could to find my buried treasure that God had hoped I would find. I took over 60 hours of teaching in seven days. Instead of being overwhelmed, as I was told I would be if I attempted that, I was experiencing complete and utter euphoria and had discovered my purpose and destiny...or at least a major part of it.

## DIALOGUING WITH GOD

My dream life became more exciting than ever! I was actually dialoguing with God while in my dreams! I would ask Him questions and He would answer me, or I would simply figure things out while in my dreams. I had a knowing while in them that God had given me the understanding. I began having dreams within dreams, and I would be given the interpretation or I would be given a "knowing" of how to interpret a particular symbol or be given a strategy of interpreting.

I continued to pursue my training through certification courses and began to teach these concepts to others. I am an avid dreamer and dream all night every night. After the first ten years of discovering dreams had meaning, I had documented and interpreted over 30,000 personal dreams in addition to the hundreds if not thousands of dreams I interpreted for others. I even participated in dream interpretation events at places like the Super Bowl.

Over time I became a trusted confidant to church leaders, pastors, business professionals, attorneys, psychologists, physicians (even a neurosurgeon), political people, famous musicians and actors, and began having enormous favor to interpret dreams for complete strangers I would encounter in stores, at events, in restaurants, and everywhere I went. It became obvious to me people were having important dreams, they were hungry to know more, they desperately needed help, and God would use even me to reach them—simply because I was willing and available. I witnessed such beautiful peace that would flood their heart when the Holy Spirit helped me give them a correct interpretation. I witnessed over and over again tears of relief, joy, and amazement as they discovered the God of the universe loved them beyond measure and cared about every detail of their life.

Looking back now, even when I had very limited information, I can see how God Himself began to give me understanding.

At the time, it seemed so simple that I quickly dismissed that I could know anything or be correct with my approach. Even after much training and practice, I've clearly discovered that *only God* is the expert, and dreams should propel you to seek Him first! The ancient Scriptures reveal that it is God's Holy Spirit who is ultimately responsible for leading you into all truth:

> *However, when He, the Spirit of **truth**, has come, He will guide you into **all truth**; for He will not speak on His own authority, but whatever He hears He will speak; and He will tell you things to come* (John 16:13).

## SEEK ONLY GOD'S APPROVAL

We as humans long so deeply to be accepted and approved that we will often doubt our own ability unless a person validates us and gives us his or her approval. God wants us to seek only *His* approval and not need the approval of a person. It's natural to want it, but an entirely different thing to need it and depend on it. God also wants us to know He speaks to *all* of us. He will reveal secrets to those who love Him and seek Him. His Word says we only know in part, which means no one person has all the answers (see 1 Corinthians 13:9,12). This book is simply meant to help you brainstorm, give you hope, and help usher you into the exciting and specific destiny God has planned just for you; it will help you discover how He may be using dreams to communicate with you. He loves you and He *will* tell you about your purpose and destiny—if you ask and seek!

I will share some things I have learned up to this point about dream interpretation, but God Himself will show you things personally about your own dreams. He will also share secrets with those of you who pursue Him! You may get pieces of the dream interpretation puzzle, too, and I hope you will also be willing to share your pieces with the rest of us. Let your knowledge be like water that flows through you to the benefit of others and does not become a stagnant pool that stops with you. Remember, we all know in part. We need to gather all the "parts" and put the pieces together to figure it out more completely. I am forever learning new things each day about dream interpretation, and God has been so merciful and loving to keep sharing things with me—even after I make a mistake! Because dreams are subjective in nature, we will all make mistakes. There are no absolutes, which is why it's vitally imperative to have a close relationship with God and knowledge of His Word if you want to be successful at dream interpretation.

With each year that passes, I will hopefully know more about interpretation and symbolism and I continue to discover better ways or new ways of doing some things. At some point, I may discover I've done some things wrong, so just remember as you read this book to keep in mind that God wants to speak to you *personally*, and do not fully trust any one person more than God if Scripture can confirm what you have been given. Also know that I write this book with a heart of love for you and love for God, and I am doing what I know to do right now, asking God to grant you discernment and grant me grace and mercy as I step out in faith.

No matter what I share with you in this book, test it against the Word of God and see if it "fits" for you. Ask God yourself. If something doesn't feel right, it probably isn't—at least for you personally—and what works for me may not work for you, so keep asking God about your own personal dream language. Just make sure it's from God's perspective and His holy and loving nature, which is revealed in the Holy Scriptures.

By the end of this book, I pray your spirit will be opened to a whole new realm of possibilities and your heart will be infused with hope as you begin to discover the immense love God has for you and what He is specifically revealing to you. He longs for an intimate relationship with you. Enjoy your dream journey!

## PROPHETS, SEERS, AND THE ROLE OF HUMILITY

As already mentioned, I have personally documented more than 30,000 dreams of my own over the course of just the first ten years of realizing dreams have meaning. I usually remember and document five to seven dreams a night, and I've probably lost more dreams than I've remembered. I dream all night, every night. Even as I begin to doze off I can enter into a dream. I've even been involved in sleep studies, and with their permission awoke several times during the night to write down my dreams! They were amazed as they discovered I never really reach the deep realm of sleep and were astonished that having so many dreams energized me instead of exhausting me.

Many years ago, God revealed to me I was a prophetic seer. I didn't even know what a seer was! I found through reading the Bible that there are prophets and seers. A seer is a type of prophet. What I believe I've learned so far is that prophets hear or see things literally and repeat exactly what they see or hear from God. Seers tend to hear, see, feel, and experience God in very symbolic and metaphorical ways, and they often have to interpret what they are experiencing in order to understand what God is trying to convey. There were eight specific seers mentioned in Scripture.

I point this out only because I believe God intentionally appoints some to hear Him more often specifically through dreams. It says in the book of Numbers, *"Then He [Lord God] said, 'Hear now My words: If there is a prophet among you, I, the Lord, make Myself known to him in a vision; I speak to him in a dream'"* (Numbers 12:6). I believe this is one reason that explains why some people remember more dreams than others. However, though it's not an absolute, I've frequently found that incredibly creative or emotional people tend to have an easier time remembering their dreams, whereas logistical people tend to remember fewer dreams—though this is not always the case. Don't be too impressed with those of us who remember more of our dreams.

God went on to say that because Moses was a faithful servant, God spoke to him face to face plainly and not in a way that had to be interpreted, because Moses was the most humble man on earth. This tells me that the more humble and the more faithful we are, the more God will speak to us plainly.

Let's take a look at the complete passage in Numbers:

> *Then He [God] said, "Hear now My words: If there is a prophet among you, I, the Lord, make Myself known to him in a vision; I speak to him in a dream. Not so with My servant Moses; he is faithful in all My house. I speak with him face to face, even plainly, and not in dark sayings; and he sees the form of the Lord. Why then were you not afraid to speak against My servant Moses?"* (Numbers 12:6-8)

Perhaps we could think about dreams as a sort of heavenly email system. God communicates with us through dream mail. Think about those you love the most—who are they? Your spouse, your parents, your children, your dearest friends and loved ones? Would you rather get an email from them or talk with them face to face? We don't always talk face to face with everyone we get emails from. We reserve that time and attention for those who are closest to us. I believe that the closer you get to God, the more obedient and humble you become, the more you will hear from Him directly and not in hidden speech and dark sayings. We will discuss why God speaks in these hidden ways a bit later in the book.

## WHY DON'T I REMEMBER MY DREAMS?

I realize science tells us we all dream, and that's true. After all, God created us and He is the one who created each of us to dream. However, one of the most frequent questions I'm asked is, "Why don't I dream?" or "Why don't I remember my dreams?" There are many answers to those questions, but I want to encourage you that God *does speak and is speaking* to you all the time—even if you aren't dreaming! Even if you don't remember your dreams, perhaps it's because God is speaking to you in yet another way more often.

Learning to interpret will help you understand a myriad of ways God speaks throughout each day and it will even open your understanding when you read the Bible. You'll begin to ask, "Why was that detail mentioned in Scripture?" or you'll begin to interpret your life as though it were a dream and discover how much more everything makes sense! We have an amazing Creator and His ways are so much higher than ours. His Word says that *all of creation speaks of Him!*

You can find more information on why we don't remember our dreams in Chapter 7, "The Impossible Dream."

## JEDI DREAM TIPS:

- Learning how to decipher what God is saying in metaphors and symbolism will also escort you into a supernatural realm of hearing Him all the time in all of life.

- God speaks to ALL of us! We just need to learn how to understand what He is saying.

- Share what you learn with others!

- Always consult the Word of God and pray to seek the truth.

- If it doesn't feel like a right interpretation, it probably isn't.

*Chapter 4*

# WHAT DREAMS MAY COME— EXCITING ADVENTURES AWAIT!

There are many reasons for dreams we will discuss and explain later, and many different types of dreams that can take you on supernatural, spiritual adventures. Even the ones we create in our subconscious can be thrilling and fun! Allow me to share just a few examples of adventures I've had in hopes it will encourage, provoke, and propel you to pay attention to your own dreams and even to ask God to speak to you this way.

## SUPERNATURAL EXPERIENCES IN DREAMS: WALKING ON THE MOON

One of my all-time favorite dreams was when I got to walk on the moon! It was an incredibly lucid dream, and it felt as real as truly being there with all my senses intact. The left side of the moon was dark, and the right side was bright. I was there alone and standing at about 10 o'clock on the dark side of the moon, and I was gazing out at the spectacular stars in total awe and wonder. I was amazed at the breathtaking beauty of how the stars were sparkling like diamonds in the night, and I was fascinated with being on the moon itself. I saw a narrow path that escalated toward the top of the dark side of the moon. I stepped onto this narrow path and knew when I got to the top it would turn bright and I would be very busy. I also knew things would get much easier because I would be going downhill instead of up. I then woke up.

The essence of the interpretation is that even though I was walking through a very dark and difficult time (the dark side of the moon), I chose to look at the beauty in it and I chose God's narrow path, which leads to life. I knew the dream was revealing that although I was going through a difficult season and there was still a little ways to go, I would eventually make it to the top (success) and things would get easier as I walked in the light, meaning God's truth. I also instinctively knew in the dream that it was important to embrace and cherish this time, though it was lonely and difficult.

## BACK TO THE FUTURE: A TIME-TRAVEL DREAM

Years ago I worked for Universal Pictures, Home Video Division. One of the movies we sold was *Back to the Future*, a story about traveling through time into the future and returning. I recently had a dream where I was taken through time and into the future of this very book! An unseen person took me into the future, and I was observing someone's private den and library. It was rather large for a personal library and it had two sections with a step up between them. I was shown my book was there on a shelf. It was a small leather-bound book that had become a classic. I saw the tip of a pair of tweezers had scratched the title into the leather. I then woke up.

### A Possible Interpretation

Prophetic dreams are hard to prove until they come to pass. Whether this dream was authored by my hopeful imagination or one that God truly gave me, we won't know until and if this book actually becomes a classic in the future. If I was to guess at the interpretation right now, I would say that God gave me the dream simply because there was an invisible Person with me. In dreams, this is usually the Holy Spirit, because He is present with you even though He is Spirit and cannot be seen. At first, I asked God if the small size of the book meant it wouldn't do well, perhaps representing a small number of sales. He then reminded me of the fact it was a classic and also pointed out the size of the library, which was unusually large. Small (the size of the book in the dream) can often represent humility, and the tweezers could represent precision and also giving people precise "tips" (I saw the tips of the tweezers). I felt these were instructions to make sure I took a humble approach (stay small) and give specific (precise) tips. Leather would probably reveal that if I follow the instructions, the book would stand the test of time.

Since the beginning of my dream training, God has constantly reminded me to teach an approach that expresses humility, leaving room to be wrong so the Holy Spirit can still bring correct interpretation to each dreamer. There are few absolutes in dream interpretation. I felt God wanted me to give you specifics so you could begin to interpret dreams on your own and seek God instead of needing someone else to interpret, as I did. We'll have to wait and see whether this is a dream authored out of the desire of my soul or one that God truly gave me. Either way, there are aspects of the dream that can be used to teach you, such as what the specific symbols may represent.

## A DREAM COME TRUE:
## A GLANCE AT PROPHETIC DREAMS

I have had hundreds of dreams come true—if not thousands. These types of dreams are called prophetic dreams. I seem to have them almost on a weekly basis for my own personal life. Prophetic dreams are difficult to discern because many times you will not know they were prophetic unless or until they come to pass, unless God reveals it to you while you're in the dream or there are elements that indicate it's from God and you know it hasn't happened yet. I believe prophetic dreams are often simply "bookmarks" letting you know you're on the right page in life.

I tend to find that I'll get prophetic dreams for myself when I'm in need of encouragement as I experience something difficult. I also get them to relieve me of worries and to confirm things God has revealed to me in Scripture or in prayer. I've received many prophetic dreams about this very book that have included encouragement for the outcome, directions for writing it, instructions for who to publish with and when, etc.

**Prophetic dreams are often "bookmarks" letting
you know you're on the right page in life.**

In one of the dreams I had, I was attending the funeral for Bob Jones, a prophet of God whom I knew. While at the funeral in the dream, an angel of God was excited I was there and took me "around the corner" to introduce me to a publisher. The publisher already had orders waiting on my book, and they were just waiting for me to finish it! When I woke up, I knew that a publishing deal was "right around the corner" from the time of Bob Jones's funeral, which was in February 2014. In March 2014, I received an email from the publisher of this book! What's difficult about prophetic dreams is that they will not always have Scripture to validate them because they are events that have not happened yet and they are not direct conversations with God, which will *always* have Scripture to validate them.

**Dreams that are conversations with God will always have Scripture to validate them.**

Sometimes there are prophetic warning dreams from God for specific people or people groups. Sometimes I get prophetic dreams for individuals I know. On about a dozen occasions, I have had very serious warning dreams from God for specific groups of people in the church, like prophets, leaders, and pastors. Several of these can be found on my website at www.gatewaytodreams .com. Two of the most significant ones I received were called "Dead Man's Curve" and "Warning for Those in Leadership." These were very important dreams directly from God that He gave me Scripture for and a mandate to release them.

## WARNING DREAMS

### Fasting 21 Days for My Son

One of the most important dreams to I've had date was one that gave me instructions on how to win a spiritual battle for one of my sons. In the dream, I was instructed to do a Daniel fast and pray for 21 days. A Daniel fast is simply a specific type of fast for 21 days, like Daniel did in the Bible for spiritual breakthrough. I had no idea what this spiritual battle was in regard to, but I paid attention to the warning! Exactly when my fast ended, my son was falsely accused of very serious charges that carried with them a prison sentence of ten years to life! The allegations were proved false within 24 hours, and I knew without a doubt that it was because God had me fasting and praying leading up to this accusation, and He answered my prayers and the prayers of those who prayed with us. I don't even want to think what would have happened had I not obeyed the warning! The enemy was obviously after my son, and God stepped in to intervene and deliver him from wicked schemes!

God loves you so much that He will give you warnings in dreams, even if you are someone who doesn't dream very often or you may not remember your dreams very often. God longs to be involved in your life and help you in every way.

I cannot begin to tell you how many prophetic warning and instruction dreams I've had about and for my children. My two sons must get very frustrated at times that God reveals their plans when they're stepping off track because He loves them so much! I've received dozens of dreams warning me what my children were up to, only to find out that they came to pass usually within a week. Why would God do that? Several reasons!

1.  So I would pray for my children to make correct choices.

2.  So I can warn them in hopes they will make different choices.

3.  To give me an opportunity to process my own emotions before it happens so I respond correctly!

I remember having a dream about one of my children, and in the dream he had done something wrong. Inside the dream I went ballistic and was screaming and yelling and was utterly dismayed. I was given instruction in the dream of what my reaction should rather be, and I simply did it. God was revealing to me that this child needed to feel loved and I was to show him my support, regardless of his behavior. I was shown to not respond how he expected me to and almost provoked me to. In reality, this happened three days later; when it happened, I wasn't taken by surprise at all—I responded instead of reacted! I have to be honest and say we were both amazed at my response. It's so incredible to me that we can get a sneak preview or an opportunity to practice before the event actually happens so we can pass the test! How cool is that! God is love. He desires to be involved in our lives if we will allow and invite Him to be.

God has also given me serious prophetic warning dreams for leaders in the church, which had many Scriptures to confirm them. You can locate these on the website, www.gatewaytodreams.com, or our Facebook page at www.facebook.com/gatewaytodreams.

## ENCOURAGEMENT DREAMS: GOD'S REMARKABLE LOVE

### Surprised by Love

I had two friends who were married to one another and had been dear friends of mine for years. They lived a couple of hours away, and I only got to see them when I would visit Columbia, South Carolina to teach on dreams. In July 2014, I had a dream that initially confused me. The husband had come to me inside the dream and told me to tell his wife he was pleased at how she had handled everything and that she was doing great! He wanted me to tell her he was proud of her! He acted as though he was looking down from Heaven at her, and he had the biggest and most beautiful smile that revealed his overwhelming love for her.

I woke up and was utterly confused! I tried for over an hour to figure out what that may have meant symbolically. I also wondered if it was something symbolic concerning me, because dreams are often about the dreamer and I had not been in contact with either of them for a few months. The last contact I had was a phone call from the husband inviting me to attend a ministry event they were hosting.

After much confusion and frustration, I simply texted him to let him know I had a dream about them and wanted to brainstorm with them in regard to what it may mean. I never heard back from him. A week went by, and as I turned on my computer one morning to check my Facebook pages, I was shocked to discover the wife had a massive stroke days prior and was in serious condition in the hospital!

At this point, I still had not gotten ahold of her husband, but I felt my dream was probably to encourage her, so I immediately began getting ahold of other people who may be able to get her the message. A mutual friend of ours conveyed the message of love from the dream for me. I presumed that the husband may have represented Jesus in the dream, because in the Bible it speaks of Jesus being the bridegroom of His bride, the church. Therefore, sometimes our spouse can represent Jesus if it's in the right context. I thought perhaps Jesus was just encouraging her that *He* was proud of her and wanted to motivate her to stay strong and that she would make it through this very difficult time.

I can't remember if it was days or weeks later, but I eventually spoke with her by phone when she was able. When I personally told her about my dream in specific detail, she informed me that her husband had gone to his cardiologist on May 8th, and on May 9th he had a heart attack and died. I couldn't believe what I was hearing! I had not known he even passed away, and God loved her so much that He gave a dream to someone who would let her know His amazing message of love for her in a time when she needed it most! I believe the dream also revealed joy in the way she was handling not only the massive stroke she just experienced, but also the passing of her beloved husband.

There is much theological debate over whether it was really her husband able to speak in a dream to me to convey a message, or if it was simply the Lord embracing her with His love in a way she needed to receive it. It doesn't really matter which it was or if it was both. The bottom line is that there is no way I knew he had died, and I got a dream that he was encouraging her from Heaven. God's love is simply immeasurable, and there are no lengths to which He will not go to reach each of us if we will receive it.

## INSTRUCTION DREAMS

Just as He often did in Scripture, God can give us instruction dreams, explaining something to us or giving us direction or specific instructions on what to do.

I had a dream years ago where God gave me understanding of what a specific Scripture in the Bible truly meant. Not only did He show me that it is one often misunderstood, but He also gave me instruction to share the meaning with others. Here is a brief synopsis of the dream:

### *"The Joy of the Lord Is Your Strength" Dream*

For years I have heard people use the phrase, "The joy of the Lord is your strength." However, every time I heard it used, the implication was that if you're going through a difficult time, the instruction was to simply worship the Lord until you had joy. The joy from worshiping would strengthen you. After this dream, I realized that's not what it means at all, even if you do gain the desired result of being strengthened from worshiping Him.

In the dream, I was attending some sort of Christian worship experience. There were presumably hundreds of people there. All of a sudden, I was what is known as "slain in the Spirit," which simply means under the power of God. While I was on the floor under the power of God, He supernaturally gave me the understanding of Nehemiah 8:10 and told me to share with others its true meaning. He wanted them to know what it truly meant, and He wanted people to realize that many of them had taken the verse out of context.

By supernatural revelation, almost as if He was downloading everything concerning this verse into my being, I realized what *"the joy of the Lord is your strength"* meant. I realized that it was not about *putting our joy in the Lord.* It is about *the joy of the Lord—His* joy in *us* when we obey Him. When we obey Him, it causes us to be strengthened because of His delight in our obedience. Again, it's not our joy in Him, but His joy in our obedience that gives us strength!

Of course, upon awakening I looked up this Scripture in its full context to see if this dream really was from the Lord. In Nehemiah, it explains how a ruined city was rebuilt. Ezra, a priest, read the Law of Moses to all the people. It says in Nehemiah 8:3, *"and the ears of all the people were attentive to the Book of the Law."* Nehemiah 8:5 reveals that when the Book of the Law was opened, all the people stood up in reverence. Nehemiah 8:6 goes on to show how the people responded with worship, with agreement, with lifting up their hands and also worshiping God with their faces to the ground, which again shows incredible reverence and a beautiful response of humility. The book of the Law of Moses was read and explained fully to them so they would understand God's ways. As they learned, they began to mourn and weep. Because they were responding to God in a reverential manner and having a change of heart, God was so pleased with them that He wanted them to know their obedience caused Him great joy and that His joy in their obedience would be what they could depend on for their strength—that God was *for* them! Instead of mourning, He wanted them to celebrate because they had hearts to obey.

Let's take a quick look:

> *And Nehemiah, who was the governor, Ezra the priest and scribe, and the Levites who taught the people said to all the people, "This day is holy to the Lord your God; do not mourn nor weep." For all the people wept, when they heard the words of the Law. Then he said to them, "Go your way, eat the fat, drink the sweet, and send portions to those for whom nothing is prepared; for this day is holy to our Lord. Do not sorrow, for the joy of the Lord is your strength." So the Levites quieted all the people, saying, "Be*

*still, for the day is holy; do not be grieved." And all the people went their way to eat and drink, to send portions and rejoice greatly, because they understood the words that were declared to them* (Nehemiah 8:9-12).

You can see that the people had the right response to God and understood the words that were given to them. Because they had a heart change, God was greatly pleased with them and wanted them to know they could be strengthened by His joy in them. Wow. Can you see how easily we can get one simple sentence wrong by not keeping it in context or by putting the emphasis on the wrong thing? Dreams are the same way. If you don't keep them in context, you will change their entire meaning. Do you see the difference? Instead of us thinking the joy of the Lord means our joy *in* Him, it really means God's joy in us—the joy *of the Lord*. I think it's totally amazing that God would personally reveal understanding of Holy Scripture in and through a dream! The ultimate message as a result of this dream is also that God wants us to obey and respond to Him, and if we do we can count on Him to be for us! He is our strength.

## FAMOUS DREAMS

Dreams have played an enormously important role in history. Without them we wouldn't have the knowledge of $E=mc^2$ or the DNA double helix, two scientific discoveries commonly said to have begun within dreams. Let's take a quick look at famous dreams throughout history to further reveal the validity and importance of dreams.

### Instruction

Golfer Jack Nicklaus, who was a six-time Masters champion, was struggling with his swing. He had a dream that gave him specific instruction on how to change his grip, and after he applied what he learned in the dream, his golf swing significantly improved.[1]

## Inventions

Madame C.J. Walker (1867–1919) is in the *Guinness Book of World Records* as the first female American self-made millionaire. She founded and built a highly successful African-American cosmetic company that made her a multi-millionaire. She said God answered her prayer to solve a problem about a scalp infection. She stated, "He answered my prayer...for one night I had a dream, and in that dream a big black man appeared to me and told me what to mix for my hair. Some of the remedy was from Africa, but I sent for it, mixed it, put it on my scalp and in a few weeks my hair was coming in faster than it had ever fallen out." She shared her remedy with others, and they too experienced great results. Eventually, she sold her product and became wealthy.[2]

## Music

- Paul McCartney composed the melody of The Beatles' song "Yesterday" from a dream in 1964.[3]

- George Frideric Handel may have been inspired by a dream to write the chorus to *Messiah*. He said of it, "I did think I did see all Heaven before me and the great God Himself."

## Medicine and Science

God can give you heavenly insight for new inventions and solutions:

- Albert Einstein's Theory of Relativity, $E=mc^2$, came in a dream that he pondered for years.

- The Periodic Table—Dmitry Mendeleyev was working furiously for three days and stopped to take a quick nap and claimed to have received the periodic table from a dream.

- Otto Loewi (1873–1961), a German physiologist, won the Nobel Prize for medicine in 1936 for his work on the chemical transmission of nerve impulses.[4]

- Some have claimed that the double helix structure of DNA was revealed through James Watson's dream of a spiral staircase.

- Friedrich Kekule invented the chemical structure of Benzene Molecule ($c6H6$) when he had a dream of a group of snakes swallowing their tails.[5]

## Books and Movies Influenced by Dreams

- Stephen King's *Misery*[6]

- Frankenstein[7]

- Inception

- Dr. Jekyll and Mr. Hyde[8]

- Twilight[9]

- Anne Rice has stated she uses dreams to write her novels.

- Author Richard Bach received the book *Jonathan Livingston Seagull* in two phases. One was a voice that whispered the title to him, and eight years after that he saw the book in a dream. It went on to become the best-selling book at the time.[10]

## Poetry

Edgar Allan Poe's nightmares inspired many of his poems and short stories. He also wrote several poems about the phenomenon of dreaming, including "Dream-Land" and "A Dream Within a Dream."

## Artwork

Child prodigy and dear friend of mine Akiane Kramarik has received inspiration for many of her paintings from dreams. I encourage you to visit her website at www.artakiane.com to view her astounding paintings, poetry, and parables. Though it was specifically inspired from an actual encounter with God and not by a dream, her rendering of Jesus is also used in the book and movie *Heaven Is for Real* as a confirmation from another child of what they experienced Jesus looking like.

Salvador Dali has called many of his pieces "hand-painted dream photographs."

## Prophetic

Abraham Lincoln dreamed of his own assassination. President Lincoln even discussed his recurring dreams with General Grant during a cabinet meeting and believed they revealed that important news from General Sherman on the front would arrive soon. Lincoln was known to value the importance of dreams.[11]

### JEDI DREAM TIPS

- Dreams that are communicating a message to you directly from God will ALWAYS have a scripture to validate them.

- Prophetic dreams are often "bookmarks" letting you know you're on the right page in life.

- Many famous movies, books, songs, and inventions came through dreams!

## ENDNOTES

1.  "Five Dream Discoveries," BBC News, June 10, 2009, The World-Class Golf Swing, accessed January 19, 2015, http://news.bbc.co.uk/2/hi/uk_news/magazine/8092029.stm.

2.  A'Lelia Bundles, *On Her Own Ground: The Life and Times of Madam C.J. Walker* (New York, NY: Scribner, 2001), 60.

3.  "Five Dream Discoveries," BBC News, June 10, 2009, The Song, accessed January 19, 2015, http://news.bbc.co.uk/2/hi/uk_news/magazine/8092029.stm.

4.  Ibid., The Nobel Prize-Winning Discovery.

5.  John Read, *From Alchemy to Chemistry* (New York, NY: Dover Publications, 1995), 174.

6.  Stephen King, "Misery," StephenKing.com, accessed January 19, 2015, http://stephenking.com/library/novel/misery_inspiration.html.

7.  "Five Dream Discoveries," BBC News, June 10, 2009, The Monster, accessed January 19, 2015, http://news.bbc.co.uk/2/hi/uk_news/magazine/8092029.stm.

8.  Michael Delahoyde, "Dr. Jekyll and Mr. Hyde," Washington State University, Background, accessed January 19, 2015, http://public.wsu.edu/~delahoyd/jekyll.html.

9.  Stephenie Meyer, "Twilight," StephenieMeyer.com, accessed January 19, 2015, http://stepheniemeyer.com/twilight.html.

10. Richard Bach, "Rarely Asked Questions: How Did Jonathan Seagull Come to You?" *Richard Bach: The Official Site* (blog), October 4, 2011, accessed January 19, 2015, http://richardbach.com/hello-world-2/.

11. "Did Abraham Lincoln Predict His Own Death?" History.com, October 31, 2012, accessed January 19, 2015, http://www.history.com/news/ask-history/did-abraham-lincoln-predict-his-own-death.

## Section 2

# ENTER THE DREAM GATE

*Chapter 5*

# THE THINGS DREAMS
# ARE MADE OF

Now that we've explored some of the incredible experiences we can have within our dreams, let's once again peer into Heaven's mysteries to see further what God has to say about the origin of dreams and their purpose.

## THE PURPOSE-DRIVEN DREAM

Even though we will prove to you scripturally that not all dreams are from God later in this chapter, God still created us with the ability to dream, so it stands to reason they all have purpose. It's incredibly cool to think that the Creator of the universe cares so much about us that He is talking to us all the time—even when we're sleeping! The sad part is most believers don't even know it, or worse, they simply refuse to believe it! Lack of faith is different from unbelief. The Bible says if you have faith as small as a mustard seed you can do amazing things! (See Matthew 17:20.) Unbelief, however, is an intentional decision not to believe. If you refuse to believe, it's a sign your heart has grown hard, and it might be why you may not hear God as often or as clearly as you could.

Let's take a closer look at the ancient path. There are several types of dreams mentioned in Scripture, and each had its own purpose. Because we will always use God's Word as our plumb line, let's see what He says about dreams:

- There can be false dreams and false dreamers (see Jeremiah 23:25-33; 27:9-10; 29:8-9; Deuteronomy 13:1-5; Jude 4-11; Zechariah 10:2). If dreams and dreamers can be false, we can deduct they can also be *true!* Proof includes prophetic dreams coming to pass, visitations from God in dreams, etc.

- We can cause ourselves to dream (see Jeremiah 29:8).

- Dreams can fly away quickly (see Job 20:4-9; Psalm 73:20). In other words, they can be difficult to recall.

- Dreams happen while sleeping (see Job 4:13; 33:15; Psalm 16:7). They are different from visions, which you may have either while awake or asleep.

- God speaks to His prophets this way (see Numbers 12:1-13).

- They are considered dark sayings from God (see Numbers 12:6-8).

- Correct interpretations belong to God (see Genesis 40:8).

- Some dreams and visions are meant to get our attention (see Job 7:13-15).

- God speaks in dreams to give instruction and keep us from pride (see Job 33:14-17).

- They can give us instructions, warnings, and provide protection (see Genesis 20:3-7; 31:10-13; 31:24-39; Daniel 4:1-28; Matthew 2:12-15;19-23).

- You can have angelic visitations or godly encounters in dreams (see Genesis 28:10-22; 1 Kings 3:5-15).

- Dreams can bring us conviction and our heart can instruct us at night (see Matthew 27:19; Psalm 16:7).

- Dreams can tell of future events (see Genesis 37:5-11; 40:5-23; 41:1-44; Daniel 2:1-45; 7:1-14).

- Much activity can cause vain dreams (see Ecclesiastes 5:3-7).

- Dreams can encourage us (see Judges 7:13-15).

- Dreams can reveal our destiny (see Genesis 37:5-11; 40:5-23).

I also believe some of our dreams come from the enemy, satan, trying to either scare us with condemnation, provoke us into pride, or he can even come as an angel of light and give us messages that seem good, but are not of God. Although this verse in Scripture is not specifically about dreams necessarily, it does demonstrate that a believer in Jesus Christ can be influenced by satan: "Then satan entered Judas, surnamed Iscariot, who was numbered among the twelve" (Luke 22:3). Judas was a disciple of Jesus, and this verse makes it clear that satan was able to influence him.

In my Dreamology® courses, we thoroughly discuss each individual dream and also the meaning behind each word used for *dream* in Scripture. You can locate the upcoming classes on our website: www.gatewaytodreams.com.

## ONCE UPON A TIME: PARABLES AND ALLEGORIES

Dreams are often parables or allegories. What is a parable? When you think of a parable, think of the word *parallel*. It's a story that parallels real life. To help you understand further, here are a few definitions for *parable* according to online dictionaries:

- A short story designed to illustrate or teach some truth, religious principle, or moral lesson; a statement or comment that conveys a meaning indirectly by the use of comparison, analogy, or the like.[1]

- A short story that uses familiar events to illustrate a religious or ethical point.[2]

It says in Matthew 13 that Jesus only spoke in parables to crowds in order to teach:

> *All these things Jesus spoke to the multitude in parables; and without a parable He did not speak to them, that it might be fulfilled which was spoken by the prophet, saying: "I will open My mouth in parables; I will utter things kept secret from the foundation of the world" (Matthew 13:34-35).*

The reason He spoke in parables is clearly stated in Scripture after Jesus had taught several parables to the crowds:

> *And the disciples came and said to Him, "Why do You speak to them in parables?" He answered and said to them, "Because it has been given to you to know the mysteries of the kingdom of heaven, but to them it has not been given. For whoever has, to him more will be given, and he will have abundance; but whoever does not have, even what he has will be taken away from him. Therefore I speak to them in parables, because seeing they do not see, and hearing they do not hear, nor do they understand. And in them the prophecy of Isaiah is fulfilled, which says: 'Hearing you will hear and shall not understand, and seeing you will see and not perceive; for the hearts of this people have grown dull. Their ears are hard of hearing, and their eyes they have closed, lest they should see with their eyes and hear with*

*their ears, lest they should understand with their hearts
and turn, so that I should heal them.' But blessed are your
eyes for they see, and your ears for they hear; for assuredly,
I say to you that many prophets and righteous men desired
to see what you see, and did not see it, and to hear what
you hear, and did not hear it"* (Matthew 13:10-17).

To recap, the reason Jesus only spoke in parables was so people would apply their hearts to understand and not just have their heads puffed up with more knowledge. To understand a parable, you have to meditate upon it to see how it is a lesson or truth that you can apply to your life. Not everyone wants to know because then they will be required to respond. Dreams are often the same way. They show you something about yourself, and you have to choose if you want to see it and decide how to respond.

Dreams are often parables and allegories to teach you something. That's why if you're dreaming a parable, you will often dream of something like work because it's something you understand. I cannot begin to tell you how many people say to me they just dream of work because they're always working. Perhaps instead it's God trying to reveal how something else is a parallel to what happens at work. For instance, maybe it's a parable that coincides with your actions or emotions at work, how to handle something in your life exactly how you would handle it at work, or maybe it simply showing you a need for a similar structure or diligence in an area of your life that you have at work. You normally don't dream of work because you work; you have work in your dreams because you understand concepts about work, and it's often being used to help you understand something else.

## Allegories

An allegory is slightly different from a parable. An allegory is more symbolic and contains things that may not really exist in life, such as talking objects, etc. One definition I think best explains an allegory is that it uses symbolism to illustrate truth or a moral.

I've had numerous allegories in my dreams containing things that either can't happen in real life or don't truly exist. One of the most fun ones I had was when I dreamt of an "ott." I explain this dream later in the book when I discuss unique symbols.

## WHY GOD COMMUNICATES SYMBOLICALLY: EXPLORING SYMBOLS AND FIGURES OF SPEECH

You may ask why God would use symbols and figures of speech to communicate with us. Why wouldn't He just speak plainly? The answer is not entirely simple, but basically God uses things you understand to explain things you don't understand. He uses the physical realm to explain the supernatural spiritual realm.

To think that God does not continue to speak symbolically or metaphorically through dreams is to deny His nature throughout Scripture—from Genesis to Revelation. God uses symbols to reveal attributes and to cause you to apply your heart to understand. Did you know there are over 8,200 figures of speech used in Scripture? That is totally amazing to me! If we know the Word of God is inspired by the Holy Spirit, then whenever symbolic speech is used in Scripture, it is on purpose and it means we should *stop and take notice and learn something.*

**God uses the things you understand to explain the things you don't. He uses the physical realm to explain the supernatural spiritual realm.**

The entire Hebrew culture celebrates and communicates through symbolic expression in their feasts, their traditions, and even every letter of their alphabet is a symbolic picture of something! I personally believe metaphors and symbolic ways of communicating are God's preferred speech because we have to *want* to understand and we have to *apply* our hearts to understand. When we learn to think symbolically, we will discover all types of hidden treasures, not only in our dreams, but more importantly in Scripture and in our everyday lives! You will begin to hear and see God communicating with you everywhere, every day, when you begin to apply your heart to understand the meaning behind God's symbolic love language.

God says to love the Lord your God with *all* of your heart, soul, and strength (see Deuteronomy 6:5; 11:13; 13:3). How can we do that unless we apply our hearts fully to understand? When we have to gain an understanding of symbols or metaphors, it requires us to meditate and involve our minds, our wills, our experiences, and our emotions—only then can we begin to understand what God is saying.

Dreams are often parables, allegories, or even riddles that contain hidden treasure if we're willing to search for it. The condition of our hearts directly affects our spiritual insight and understanding. Are you distracted or captivated by the gift God may be giving you in your dreams? It may reflect the condition of your heart.

Jesus spoke in parables to the unbelieving because He wanted them to have to apply their hearts. He says:

> *This is why I speak to them in parables: "Though seeing, they do not see; though hearing, they do not hear or understand." In them is fulfilled the prophecy of Isaiah: "You will be ever hearing but never understanding; you will be ever seeing but never perceiving. For this people's heart has become calloused; they hardly hear with their ears, and they have closed their eyes. Otherwise they might see with their*

*eyes, hear with their ears, understand with their hearts and turn, and I would heal them"* (Matthew 13:13-15 NIV).

Jesus goes on to bless those who listen and apply themselves to understand what He is saying. Notice, too, that He explained what the parables meant to the disciples who asked (those who want to know!). To be a disciple means to study and follow Jesus. When He speaks symbolically, it means there is hidden treasure to be discovered, and those who search it out will find reward! (See Matthew 7:7; Luke 11:9; Hebrews 11:6.)

E.W. Bullinger, who was a biblical scholar and theologian from England in the late 1800s, gives us the following for serious reflection in his book, *Figures of Speech Used in the Bible*:

> Applied to words, a figure denotes some form which a word or sentence takes, different from its ordinary and natural form. This is always for the purpose of giving additional force, more life, intensified feeling, and greater emphasis. Whereas today "Figurative language" is ignorantly spoken of as though it made less of the meaning, and deprived the words of their power and force. A passage of God's Word is quoted; and it is met with the cry, "Oh, that is figurative"— implying that its meaning is weakened, or that it has quite a different meaning, or that it has no meaning at all. But the very opposite is the case. For an unusual form (*figura*) is never used except to add force to the truth conveyed, emphasis to the statement of it, and depth to the meaning of it. When we apply this science then to God's words and to Divine truths, we see at once that no branch of Bible study can be more important, or offer greater promise of substantial reward.[3]

Bullinger goes on to say, referring to figures of speech, "no branch of Bible study can be more important: and yet we may truly say that there is no branch of it which has been so utterly neglected."[4]

God is speaking to you today and desiring for you to find hidden rewards. Will you seek Him with all your heart, or will you squander your riches? It is my prayer that you will consider the condition of the soil of your heart and value how God may be communicating with you in dreams and also in everything around you. Apply your heart to understand what He may be saying, and you will be rewarded above and beyond all you can ask or even possibly imagine (see Ephesians 3:20; Hebrews 11:6).

## DISPELLING THE MYTH OF PIZZA AND BAD BURRITOS

Okay, time to take a pop quiz:

**Where do dreams come from?**

   A.  Pizza

   B.  Bad burritos

   C.  Chili-cheese dogs

   D.  None of the above

The answer is D—none of the above!

While it is possible for pain in our body to induce a dream, I think one of the reasons people like to blame dreams on food is because if it's just food then they can disammiss them as nonsense they don't have to pay attention to. Interpreting dreams can take work and it may require us to respond, and I believe that's why most people don't pay attention to their dreams. Another reason is that they have simply never been told that dreams really do matter!

## BODY, SOUL, AND SPIRIT

The Bible tells us that we are made up of body, soul, and spirit (see 1 Thess. 5:23). This topic is much deeper than we will dig into here, but dreams ultimately come from one of three places. Let's take a quick glance at these.

### The Body

We discuss the body in other places in this book, but to give you a brief overview, aches and pains, illnesses, diseases, and medications in our body can influence our dream life. If you are in severe pain, you may dream you're in severe pain or you may have what seem like nightmares. Medications can also severely affect your dreams, as discussed later in the section on nightmares.

### The Soul

The soul is also comprised of three facets—mind, will, and emotions. Dreams can come from all three of these facets. Most dreams come from our psyche or soul. I believe one of the main reasons God created us with the ability to dream is to give us a safe place to process our emotions. Most dreams are simply processing dreams, which is precisely why psychologists and psychiatrists analyze dreams. The chemicals in our brains that are attached to our emotions create pictures, and that's what we are seeing in most of our dreams. Analyzing our dreams can give us insight as to what we are having difficulty processing at a subconscious level. *Sub* means "below." We have a lot of things we process "below" the surface of our waking emotions.

I also believe many dreams are simply our conscience convicting us of what we know to be right or wrong. The caution with the conscience is that it can be seared or it can grow dull if we continually ignore promptings from God's Holy Spirit. First Timothy 4:1-2 says, "Now the Spirit expressly says that in latter times some will depart from the faith, giving heed to deceiving spirits and doctrines of demons." The amazing thing is that by a decision of our will, we can decide to renew our mind and read the Word of God and begin again! Psalm 95:8 and Hebrews 3:8 reminds us to not harden our hearts.

Scripture even reveals we can cause ourselves to dream from the desires of our own heart. It says in Jeremiah:

> For thus says the Lord of hosts, the God of Israel: Do not let your prophets and your diviners who are in your midst deceive you, nor listen to your dreams which **you** cause to be dreamed. For they prophesy falsely to you in My name; I have not sent them, says the Lord (Jeremiah 29:8-9).

The desires of our own hearts can cause us to dream what we *want* to dream. Strong emotions create vivid dreams.

Have you ever gone to bed and your mind was still rapidly searching through all the events of the day or you couldn't stop thinking about an issue, an event, or a relationship? Sometimes our mind can create dreams in order to visually deal with things. In Ecclesiastes 5:3 it states, "For a dream comes through much activity, and a fool's voice is known by his many words." This reveals that we often process things in our dreams when we are overly active.

### The Spirit: Both Good and Evil

Our dreams are often a blank canvas for the spirit realm to communicate with us. Let's take a brief look at how God communicates in dreams and how He desires to infiltrate our dream camp.

God can and does still speak to us in dreams today. It says in Joel 2:28-29 and Acts 2:17-18 that God will cause everyone to have dreams and visions. One of the most fascinating things I love about dreams is that it doesn't matter who you are or where you live, God can reach absolutely everyone through dreams because we all sleep! In fact, about a third of our life is spent sleeping.

The first dream mentioned in Scripture is in the very first book, Genesis; and the last book of the Bible, Revelation, is one big vision! Dreams also surround the birth, life, and death of Jesus Christ. God is the same yesterday, today, and forever, and He still speaks in dreams! God clearly used dreams to speak to people throughout Scripture. Even angels showed up in dreams to give announcements and warnings to people—even unbelievers!

The enemy of our soul also uses a couple of ways to influence and invade our dream life. One way is by infiltrating dreams and turning them into nightmares causing fear, guilt, or shame. The other way is a subtle tactic to appear good so we'll think the dream is from God, but ultimately we will be misled or deceived. Scripture tells us satan can even appear as an angel of light! (See Second Corinthians 11:14.) Angels are messengers, and light often represents the truth, so satan likes to mislead people with messages that appear as the truth or good but are in actuality lies meant to deceive and derail people from God's plans. Not everything that seems good is God! We have to remember that satan doesn't show up with horns and a pitchfork. He comes in insidious ways, much like a terrorist who uses women and children to smuggle bombs, appearing innocent and unnoticeable when in fact the motive is to kill, steal, and destroy. One of his favorite tactics is to provoke your pride and get you to think you're missing out on something—just as he did with Eve in the Garden of Eden.

## TYPES OF DREAMS

We've already discovered where dreams come from and why God speaks symbolically, so let's take a quick look at what ancient Scripture says about the types of dreams we have. After studying the dreams in the Bible, I've discovered they all fall into one of six categories. We teach on this topic in much more depth in our Dreamology courses listed on our website, and you can find the info in the back pages of this book. Other people may categorize these in different ways, but these essentially cover the basics. Let's take a quick look:

## Encouragement Dreams

These are dreams that give us hope, encourage us we're on the right track, bring emotional healing, etc. Some of these dreams may also be grouped under prophetic dreams if they are encouragement of things to come.

## False Dreams

These dreams are not from God. They can come from a variety of sources:

- People who appear godly, but in reality have false motives. Sometimes they are prophets who have gone astray.

- Dreamers who have caused themselves to dream something they desire.

- The enemy (satan) packaged in disguise in an attempt to deceive you from God's plans for your life.

## Instruction Dreams

These can be dreams from God, angels, the Holy Spirit, or our sanctified conscience giving us specific instruction on what, how, where, why, or when to do something.

## Processing Dreams

These are the majority of dreams we have! They come from our mind, will, and emotions. Dreams provide a safe place to process things we're experiencing or issues we're dealing with. They have enormous meaning and can help us understand what's going on inside our hearts.

## Prophetic Dreams

*Prophetic* simply means something that God has revealed to someone that has not happened yet. It may have conditions with it, such as repentance, or it may be a promise from God; it may require certain things from us such as obedience, etc.

I want to clarify that the prophetic is severely different from what a fortune-teller or psychic does. God says fortune-telling is detestable and He hates it! Even if the person seems good, nice, or religious, the bottom line is a fortune-teller gets the information from the wrong source—the enemy, who is satan. It can seem like the person knows the future, but only God knows the future. If you pay attention, the focus is mostly on the past to make you think the fortune teller knows things, when in reality it's just a demonic network telling him or her what has already happened. The person may tell you things about the future, but it is declaring things they want to happen instead of what God wants for you. God is the only one who can tell you about the future accurately, and He does it with enormous love and purpose.

God and satan are sending out signals—what is your radio frequency set at and which signals are you getting? If you feel you're just getting a lot of static and confusion, perhaps you just need to dial into God's Word to gain some clarity.

## Warning Dreams

These can be dreams from God, angels, the Holy Spirit, the enemy, or our own conscience warning us of choices, danger, etc. These dreams can also be grouped under prophetic dreams, because they may be warning us of things that have not happened yet but are to come.

## JEDI DREAM TIPS

- All dreams have purpose because God created us with the ability to dream and He does nothing without purpose.

- Dreams are spiritual treasure hunts to discover hidden messages.

- God uses things you understand to explain things you don't.

- Dreams are often parables, allegories, or riddles.

- Dreams can come from our body, soul, or spirit.

### ENDNOTES

1. *Dictionary.com*, s.v. "Parable," accessed January 20, 2015, http://dictionary.reference.com/.

2. *The Free Dictionary*, s.v. "Parable," accessed January 20, 2015, http://www.thefreedictionary.com.

3. E.W. Bullinger, *Figures of Speech Used in the Bible* (Grand Rapids, MI: Baker Book House, 1968), Introduction, accessed January 20, 2015, http://www.figuresofspeechinthebible.net/wp-content/uploads/2014/01/Introduction-to-Figures-Of-Speech-In-The-Bible-by-E-W-Bullinger1.pdf.

4. Ibid.

Chapter 6

# NIGHTMARES ON ELM STREET

## EXPLORING THE PURPOSE OF NIGHTMARES

Nightmares are some of the most difficult dreams to sort through. First, we have to understand what a true nightmare is. Most people will call any unpleasant dream a nightmare. I have personally come to categorize a true nightmare as one that has been given by the enemy of our soul, satan. These true nightmares are usually ones where you're being chased or choked or killed, there's a ton of absolute fear, and there's no hope of escape until you awake to find out it was just a dream. The amazing thing about these true types of nightmares is that we are allowed to see them for a purpose. By understanding satan's plans and what his intentions are, you can pray to intervene and stop them or change the outcome! I've even been able to teach people to be aware that if they dream these types of dreams, they can call out the name of Jesus and the nightmare usually stops immediately because God will intervene if you ask Him to. The mighty name of Jesus is the only name that will work for this type of spiritual warfare. God says if we will call upon the name of the Lord—and His name is *Jesus*—then we shall be saved! (See Acts 2:21; Joel 2:32.)

This chapter will review many different types of dreams that seem like nightmares. We will discuss their origin and/or their purpose. It's my hope you will discover some of your unpleasant dreams that feel like nightmares actually exist to help you work through issues, warn you of danger, and give you heavenly blueprints that reveal strategies to defeat your spiritual enemy. Let's take a look at a few categories most people consider nightmares that actually have meaning and purpose.

## Psycho: Drugs and Dreams

While holding dream interpretation events or courses, it never fails that I encounter people who struggle consistently with horrific nightmares. I've discovered, after many years of interpreting dreams, that another source of legitimate nightmares is prescription medications. Medical doctors have concluded that many drugs that act on chemicals in the brain cause nightmares, especially for adults taking certain medications.

According to WebMD, "Drugs that act on chemicals in the brain, such as antidepressants and narcotics, are often associated with nightmares."[1] The website also states that "non-psychological medications, including some blood pressure medications, can also cause nightmares."[2] The article goes on to state that another contributing factor to nightmares is "withdrawal from medications and substances, including alcohol and tranquilizers. If you notice a difference in your nightmare frequency after a change in medication, talk with your doctor."[3]

A serious consideration for why some drugs induce nightmares is because many drugs are biblically considered sorcery, which was used to allow evil spirits to control a person. There is one Hebrew word used in Scripture for sorcery and three Greek words, one of which is *pharmakeia*, which is the word we use to get our word pharmacy or pharmaceuticals—drugs and medications! I personally believe that some medications (though hear me clearly—not all!) actually open you up to the demonic realm giving them spiritual permission and control over your mind, and I believe that's what *some* nightmares are if you're on medication or using other legal or illegal substances.

### Recurring Dreams

I have personally found that recurring dreams (and nightmares) usually fall into one of two categories. The first and most common reason we have recurring dreams is because we are having a difficult time with an issue and haven't resolved processing it yet. Many times these encompass regrets, fears, traumas, worries, etc.

The second most common reason we tend to have recurring dreams is because God or our own conscience is trying to get our attention and warn us or caution us to make different choices. If they are from God, it's His amazing grace to give us many chances to deal with an issue, making sure we understand and are given the opportunity to change the outcome. If it's from the source of our conscience, then it's usually a healthy guilt or conviction that helps get us back on the right path.

On the other hand, the enemy of our soul, satan, can also influence our dream life, as discussed further in the upcoming section called "Star Wars." After years of interpreting nightmares for people, I've often found that satan will go after people who have a prophetic spiritual gift of dreaming to keep them from liking their dreams, thereby discouraging them from pursuing what they are created by God to enjoy. He frequently goes after children, too, in order to instill fear in them at a young age and try to keep them in bondage their whole life.

As I've previously mentioned, one of the number-one ways to stop some nightmares—especially for children, though it works for everyone—is to teach people to tell themselves that when they are having a nightmare, especially a recurring one, simply call out the name *Jesus* while they are in their dream, and the enemy usually disappears! The Bible says that the name of Jesus is above every name and that there will be a day when every knee bows to Him (see Phil. 2:10). When we call out the name of Jesus, it allows and invites Him into the situation and He can then help us! We were created with free will, and that is why God waits for an invitation—otherwise it wouldn't be free will.

You don't have to be in a dream to call on the name of Jesus! You can even do it right now. Simply say, "Jesus, I want to know You more and I need You in my life," and He will flood your life with love and peace. He longs to help you and usher you into your divine destiny!

## SCARY DOESN'T ALWAYS MEAN BAD!

I would venture to say that all people have, at one time or another, been awakened with dreams that seemed like nightmares, causing our heart to palpitate, our breath to quicken, and our mind to race frantically. The ironic thing is that the purpose of some dreams that seem scary may be to alert us about important things, such as the following:

*Upcoming events that may end poorly if right decisions are not made.*

These types of dreams will cause us to feel convicted about something specific we know we're doing or are planning to do that we shouldn't. This is your conscience and/or God trying to save you from consequences of a poor decision.

*The plans of the enemy who wants to steal, kill, and destroy you!*

These dreams usually reveal calamity, disaster, etc., and the purpose for you being allowed to see the plans of the enemy is so you can *pray* and ask God to intervene. Jesus says in the Word of

God, "The thief [satan] does not come except to steal, and to kill, and to destroy. I [Jesus] have come that they [you] may have life, and that they [you] may have it more abundantly" (John 10:10). See! God's plans for you are *good!* He wants you to have an *abundant life!* Jesus points out in this verse that satan's only plan is to ruin you—and God wants to stop that!

### Prophetic dreams will reveal upcoming events to you.

Sometimes events will be unavoidable, but you can get prepared by praying and studying what God says about them. I've had hundreds of these dreams, and they always gave me a distinct advantage! For example, I've had many dreams about difficult issues with my children. My prayers did not stop some of the events from happening, but while I was in the dream I got all my "freaking out" done and was shown what to do and how to handle it; then when it came to pass, I didn't freak out at all because I had already experienced it and had time to calm myself down and respond correctly! Isn't God simply *amazing?* What a gift it is to work through difficult things so you can pass the test when it comes! Other events in prophetic dreams may be completely avoidable with prayer and correct choices.

### Sometimes scary dreams are just processing scary emotions.

I've often found that if an emotion is repeatedly mentioned throughout the dream, it's often the dreamer processing a major emotion they're having trouble working through, such as fear or anger. An example of noticing this in a dream is to watch for a pattern of the same emotion. It may be the same word or different words to describe the same emotion, such as:

- "I was afraid."

- "And then I was gripped with fear."

- "It was scary."

## SEX DREAMS

Most people will at some point in their life experience a dream with sex in it. I've heard some teach that we are to "flush" these types of dreams. As I've stated already, if God created us with the ability to dream, I believe all dreams have purpose—no matter who authors the dreams. If details are there, they have purpose!

Personally, I have interpreted hundreds of dreams for others that included sex in them. All types of sex—opposite sex, extramarital sex, homosexual sex, marital sex, etc. I've endured hearing many disgusting dreams, and without fail I have discovered profound meaning to these types of dreams. It is true that some are because the person has simply been in a wrong environment, and that is referred to as "getting slimed" or coming into contact with people or places that entertain evil spirits. However, once we learn to interpret sex dreams, it will be easier to detect the ones that simply don't make sense, especially after evaluating events that have taken place in our life in proximity to the dream occurring.

To find out specifics about these types of dreams, go to Chapter 11 under Sexual Dreams.

## STAR WARS: SUPERNATURAL
## SPIRITUAL BATTLES IN DREAMS

The prominent characters in the epic movie series *Star Wars* are Luke Skywalker and Darth Vader, among many others. As you may be aware, Luke represents good or light and Darth Vader represents dark or evil. Over the years, I have discovered that people who have made the spiritual choice to make Jesus their Lord and Savior tend to experience supernatural dreams where true spiritual warfare takes place on a supernatural level. I've also encountered those who delve into darkness and have supernatural evil encounters. (To make Jesus your personal Lord and Savior, see Chapter 10,

"The Secret Gateway: Invite the Light." Few find this narrow path, but those who do experience supernatural, amazing adventures of love, peace, and power. Would you let me know if you make this decision so I can pray for you? Just go to our website at www .gatewaytodreams.com or email us at invitethelight@gatewayto dreams.com. Thank you.)

Let me share an amazing example, from a friend, of how God can give a warning dream that is really spiritual warfare and is intended to provoke prayer to change the outcome. My friend had gone to bed as usual. At one o'clock in the morning, she was awakened from a devastating dream in which she saw her son in a horrible car accident. As he came to an intersection, he was hit head-on by another car, and he died in the dream. She immediately got out of bed and got on her knees and began to pray until she had peace. She asked God to change the outcome and intervene and send angels to place a hedge of protection around him. She then went back to sleep and had a similar dream, except this time she was in the dream; when she saw her son's car coming, she—as can only be done in dreams—pushed the car out of the way and he survived in the dream.

At 3 A.M., her phone actually rang. It was the hospital calling, and her heart pounded as the person explained that her son was there being checked out—he had been in a car accident, but was miraculously uninjured. Later, when she asked the police to explain what happened, they described how supernatural it was that he survived and that his car was at a bizarre angle when they found it—had it not been for that, he would have been killed instantly. They said it didn't make sense; he should have died. When they showed her the photos from the scene, she shook. The car was exactly as it was in her dream, including the angle of his car at impact after she had pushed it—matching the dream exactly. God revealed to her that her prayers changed the outcome of satan's plans for her son's life and that God gave her the dream to encourage her that her prayers were powerful and effective. I believe that her prayers directly caused angels to push the car how it needed to be for her son to survive. When she noted the time of the crash, it happened right after her prayers!

Throughout the Bible, dreams were significant and caused incredible turning points throughout history. Dreams and visions are cited in ancient Scripture from Genesis all the way through and including the entire book of Revelation! To dismiss dreams as psychobabble or bad burritos is to dismiss that God gave us the ability to dream, and it contradicts the fact He is the same yesterday, today, and forever and can speak any way He chooses. Don't reduce God to burritos!

## THE DARK NIGHT

One of the myths I've unraveled over the years from interpreting thousands of my own dreams is that when a dream is dark, it's not necessarily bad or from the enemy. I've heard some people teach that dark dreams are soul dreams. I simply have not found that to be true! I have clearly been shown by God that sometimes dark dreams just mean it's either a feeling of darkness or a difficult time, like depression, or it may simply mean truth or "light" is lacking in the dreamer's life, just as light may be lacking in the dream. It can sometimes represent darkened thinking, too, which basically means the same thing. Most of my dreams that are dark or dimly lit in nature simply mean more understanding is needed in a situation. Truth is symbolized by light, so a lack of light simply means a lack of understanding or a lack of truth.

Another reason for darkness in a dream may be revealing a Bible verse that has the word dark, darkness, or night, etc., in it. An obvious interpretation, especially if it's very dark, is evil. The events, circumstances, and situations in the dream will help you determine how to interpret it.

## DANGER, WILL ROBINSON!

Many years ago in the 1960s, there was a television show called *Lost in Space*. One of the characters was a robot that acted as a surrogate guardian to a young boy named Will Robinson. Whenever the boy was unaware of an impending threat, the robot would say, "Warning, Will Robinson! Warning!" to alert him to the danger so he could avoid it.

Many of our dreams that feel like nightmares serve that very purpose—to warn us of danger and how to avoid it. There were many warning dreams in ancient Scripture that warned of danger and allowed people to make different choices. Some were forthtelling about the immediate or current happenings, and others were foretelling about things to come in the future.

Warning dreams are easy to detect. I have discovered at least two types of warning dreams. The first one usually contains some kind of danger you're already aware of in real life, and either a choice is given in the dream that needs to be made, or a choice is already made in the dream and you are able to see the outcome and know if it was the correct choice or not. The second kind of warning dream I often encounter is a warning dream from God about things to come. These types of dreams are usually very clear or lucid, and they usually catch you off guard because it's about the future and not about something you're aware of. The purpose of these dreams is to reveal the plans of the enemy so you can be alert to your choices and also so you can pray to God the Father and ask Him for strategy. Ask Him to intervene and stop the plans of the enemy or give you strategy to walk through it.

Sometimes the ending of a dream may not be meant to change. I have a friend who has a real heart to pray for people. People who devote themselves to pray for others are called intercessors. They intercede and pray on behalf of other people. This friend frequently has dreams from God revealing difficult things that are happening to people or are about to happen, such as death, adultery, etc. Sometimes her prayers help people through tough issues, such as adultery in a marriage. Other times, she is shown someone who is going to die and prayer will not prevent it, but her prayer will sometimes help them get right with God before they do die and/or her prayers may help the family cope with the coming devastation. Most people would lump these types of dreams in the nightmare category, when in fact they are precious gifts that allow prayer to perhaps change an outcome or provide prayer covering for those who have to deal with difficult circumstances ahead.

## BODY TRAUMA

Another significant area that can cause what we perceive as nightmares is pain, body aches, and trauma. Severe pain sends signals to our brains and can induce nightmares. Our emotions cause chemical reactions that play out as pictures in our brains. When we are sleeping and having pain, it stands to reason that the pictures that play out in our dreams are the pain we are actually experiencing, which usually appear as nightmares.

Trauma in life can also create incredible nightmarish dreams. Once again, most dreams are emotions playing out on a subconscious level, so when we are sleeping we often replay the traumatic events over and over in order to try to process them. Because there are pictures attached to our emotional chemicals in the brain, the trauma is played out in our mind's eye as a horror film. Many people who struggle with post-traumatic stress disorder (PTSD) often replay the horrific experiences they've endured.

 JEDI DREAM TIPS

- Pray and ask God to heal you of emotional distress and bring peace.

- Evaluate any medications you are taking or any illegal drug use.

- Scary does not necessarily mean bad.

- Watch for warnings in your dreams!

- Call on the name of Jesus while in a nightmare!

- Sexual dreams are rarely what you think they are!

- Darkened dreams are not necessarily soul dreams. They can sometimes simply reveal a lack of truth or understanding.

- Nightmares can often reveal the plans of satan so you can pray to prevent them.

## ENDNOTES

1.  "Adult Nightmares: Causes and Treatments," WebMD, What Causes Nightmares in Adults?, accessed January 18, 2015, http://www.webmd.com/sleep-disorders/guide/nightmares-in-adults.

2.  Ibid.

3.  Ibid.

# Chapter 7

# THE IMPOSSIBLE DREAM

Sometimes we struggle with furiously frustrating issues that seem to make it impossible to either remember our dreams or be able to figure them out because they're so long. Let's take a look at some of the issues:

- Not being able to remember them. They seem to vanish and are "gone with the wind."

- How to dissect the four-hour drama dreams that are sagas like *Gone with the Wind*.

- Struggling with deep sleep.

One of the biggest complaints I hear from people when teaching seminars and workshops is they have a difficult time remembering their dreams and wonder why. The other major frustration people seem to have frequently is they have extensively long saga dreams and don't know where to begin to interpret them. Let's take a brief look at all three issues:

## GONE WITH THE WIND: WHEN YOU CAN'T REMEMBER YOUR DREAMS

Obviously, it is important to remember your dreams so you can connect with God and enjoy communicating with Him. But have you ever had what seemed like an eternal night of dreaming, only to awake without being able to remember any of it—but still knowing you dreamt? Sometimes our dreams seem to fly away. The Bible characterizes dreams flying away as a common issue. Many dreams are like that—they fly away and are quickly forgotten, and for many reasons including not valuing dreams, being suddenly awakened, and sometimes there is simply no need to recall some dreams.

**It's important to expect to dream.
Expectation is faith!**

One reason we don't remember our dreams is that we don't value them. If we are not expecting to remember our dreams, we will automatically disregard anything we dreamt and consider it irrelevant. It's important to *expect* to dream. Expectation is *faith!* The Bible says in Hebrews 11:1, "Now faith is the substance of things hoped for, the evidence of things not seen." Faith has creative power! There is a saying, "You get what you expect, and if you don't expect much, you'll get it every time!"

## HOW TO REMEMBER MORE DREAMS

### Value your dreams—Proclaim, Prepare, and Pray!

*Proclaim!* To begin to value your dreams, first *proclaim* to yourself they are important because God gave you the ability to dream!

*Prepare!* The second important thing to do is *prepare with expectation.* How do you do that? It's incredibly simple! Simply place a notepad or paper or an electronic device next to your bed with a pen or pencil and a light. I used to use a little clip light that I could turn on in the middle of the night that wouldn't wake anyone else up, or I used the light from my phone. Now I often write my dreams with my finger on my iPad. The nice thing about using a tablet is that it is lit up already, so you don't need an extra light and all your dreams can be saved online so you can access them from any of your devices. If you're in the United States, most dollar stores have clamp lights that are portable, bendable, and the best part, only a dollar, which is cheaper than the batteries in them. Next, also *prepare* your mind to expect to dream. When I lay down to sleep, I tell myself I'm going to dream; then it's as if, while my eyes are closed, I look through my eyelids and start looking for my dream before I ever fall asleep. Many times I can enter into a dream as soon as I begin to doze off.

*Pray!* Ask God to give you dreams. Also tell yourself the ones you are causing yourself to dream can be important. Psychologists often use dreams to help counsel people through issues or trauma. Even though most of our dreams are simply us processing our emotions, they still have incredible meaning that will help us figure out what we are having issues with at a subconscious level. It can also be our conscience trying to get our attention. Much more about this is explored in coming chapters. The important part here is to pray to God for His dreams for you.

### Wake up gently.

It's very important to try and wake up gently without an alarm clock if it all possible. Alarm clocks tend to disrupt your dream state and immediately erase or delete them. Any time you are jarred out of sleep abruptly, your brain simply refocuses its attention on the urgent matter at hand. It's truly remarkable that if you tell yourself to wake up at a certain time, you will begin to do so.

You also need to anticipate giving yourself enough time to write the dream down before you have to rush and get ready to start your day. One thing I recommend if you don't have the time to write the entire dream out—either dictate it into an app that will type it for you or simply make a list of bullet points about the dream. Your brain is a network of thoughts, and if you simply jot down a few main points about the dream it will jar your memory and help to recall the entire dream for you later when you do have time to write it down.

Ancient Hebraic scrolls reveal that Daniel wrote his dreams down, telling the main facts, "In the first year of Belshazzar king of Babylon, Daniel had a dream and visions of his head while on his bed. Then he wrote down the dream, telling the main facts" (Daniel 7:1). I believe that's what bullet points can do for you— tell the main or most important facts about the dream. There are many important things to observe about this verse; however, right now the focus is to grab the main truths of the dream—the main issues, the main problems or situations, the main emotions, etc. You will learn later how to use the T.E.A. (Titles, Emotions, Actions) template as your bullet point guide. These three steps will help you simplify how to recall and interpret your dreams.

God also gave a vision to a man in the Bible named Habakkuk and told him, "Write the vision and make it plain on tablets, that he may run who reads it" (Habakkuk 2:2). In stressing the importance of writing your dreams down, we can see that Habakkuk was to make the vision *plain* on tablets. From this verse we learn: 1) it's very important to write things down that God gives you; and 2) to make something plain means to clarify it.

### No need to recall.

I believe another reason we don't remember our dreams is because sometimes we simply don't need to! I'm convinced if we don't need to process through issues, emotions, or problems, we may not need to remember our dreams. When we do remember our dreams, they are noteworthy; and when we don't remember them, we often don't have to pay attention to them. We must remember that God is faithful, and if there's something He wants to bring to our attention, there will be many other confirmations. Please know that I am careful to say that I believe it's important to *want* to remember them and attempt to recall them.

## SOAP OPERA DREAMS

Have you ever had a dream that seemed to go on and on and on? Did it remind you of a movie like *Gone with the Wind* that lasts four hours? Many dreams can have what I call multiple scenes and/ or story lines, like a movie or a soap opera has. The sheer content of these dreams can cause a person to feel incredibly overwhelmed and wonder, *Where do I even begin to interpret this dream?*

I remember years ago, when I was learning to interpret dreams, I would strive to avoid interpreting the long dreams and quickly run to the short ones, thinking the short ones would be easier. Long dreams can be intimidating because all the details can be distracting and overwhelming. But after forcing myself to study longer dreams, I began to see a pattern that was incredibly encouraging! I began to discover the longer ones were usually easier to interpret because they basically repeated the same theme over and over. Some of them simply explained the same concept or theme in several different ways so I could understand. Also, with longer dreams it's easier to find patterns of words that repeat, unique symbols or similar symbols, etc.

Many dreams will have four or five dream scenes. The easiest way to begin breaking down saga dreams is to give each scene two or three titles each and then interpret the titles. You will often find different scenes in a long dream repeatedly cover the same issue or topic.

## SLEEPING BEAUTY—DEALING WITH DEEP SLEEP

*Exhaustion can play a major role in our ability to recall our dreams.* We can also get trapped in a deep slumber due to the influence of medications or illegal drugs. Sleep medications can greatly affect your ability to recall your dreams as a result of being so deeply submersed in sleep. As discussed in Chapter 6, medications and drugs may also increase nightmares. Illegal drugs can also significantly contribute to deep sleep that prevents you from remembering your dreams, and stimulants can severely affect your sleep cycles.

## THE FAST AND THE CURIOUS

Many times I will awaken and know I've dreamed, but curiously can't immediately recall it. It's as though the feeling of the dream remains and the details quickly vanished. I've discovered that if I take a few moments to try to ease back into the dream a little, a thought or symbol will come to me from the dream and I'm able to "grab" the entire dream. (Make sure to have a backup plan for waking up on time for work in case you accidentally fall completely asleep again!)

## TOTAL RECALL

It's amazing how more of the dream will reveal itself as I'm faithful to write down even one simple word. As I've already stated, our brain is a network of associations, so when we are faithful to write down one thing, it will often connect with more associations, such as thoughts and ideas that stem from each symbol, often bringing the entire dream back to the forefront of our memory. I've also discovered many times, as I'm about to lay down for the night, the dreams from earlier that morning will return to my memory, as if my brain is trying to pick up where it left off.

Another thing that frequently seems to happen to me is that if I cannot recall the dream when I first wake up, I'll begin to go about my day and encounter something in real life that will trigger a memory, and the entire dream will be recalled! An example would be remembering a dream where I was brushing my hair or teeth as I am actually brushing my hair or teeth in real life. I would not be surprised if you have encountered the same thing!

## JEDI DREAM TIPS

- Long dreams sometimes simply repeat one main theme or issue. They can also reveal issues in several different ways through several different scenes.

- Value your dreams by proclaiming, preparing, and praying!

- Pause before you fully wake up and then write your dreams down.

- Exhaustion, medications, or illegal drugs can interfere with remembering your dreams.

- Try to ease back into the dream to reclaim details of it.

# THE DREAM MATRIX: CHOOSE WHICH APPROACH YOU WILL USE

*Chapter 8*

# STOP! BEFORE YOU BEGIN: THINGS YOU NEED TO KNOW

I know you're excited and want to jump in and find hidden treasures, but before we dive into interpreting your dreams, there are some important safety measures we need to take to ensure your dream journey is a safe and successful one! We will explore the basics of prayer and grace as well as other foundational concepts such as anchors, absolutes, dream patterns, and dream dictionaries. Let's begin!

## EAT, PRAY, LOVE...AND DREAM

### *Eat*

When you're hungry, you eat! If you are hungry to know what your dreams mean, you will have to feed your mind and apply yourself to understand. As I repeatedly mention, I believe the number-one reason God speaks symbolically is because you have to apply your heart to understand. Whatever you feed grows stronger, whether it's your mind with knowledge, your body with food, or your spirit with the Word of God. If you want to become more successful at dream interpretation, you will have to feed on the Word of God to strengthen your spiritual understanding of not only this incredible gift God has given us—called dreams—but also God's unique and amazing symbolic way of communicating with you.

## Pray

God wants you to understand! The first thing to do when you begin the interpretation of a dream is to simply pray first and ask God for help. To pray means to talk to God. Just say, "God, thank You for dreams! I really want to know what this dream means. Will You please help me understand what it means, why I had it, and if or how I'm supposed to respond to it? Thank You!" Not all dreams are from God, so you need His help knowing the source and also the correct interpretation and response. The Bible says in the book of Genesis that correct interpretations belong to God alone.

> *And they said to him* [Joseph, a dream interpreter], *"We each have had a dream, and there is no interpreter of it." So Joseph said to them, "Do not interpretations belong to God? Tell them to me, please"* (Genesis 40:8).

Only God can truly help you become more accurate. Most dreams come from our soul, and anyone with a little training in metaphorical thinking and some common sense can figure them out. However, there are some dreams that come from God, and unless He has allowed the dreamer to understand it, it will take a Christian who is a true servant of God, who has the Spirit of God, to understand what He is saying. It is very important to distinguish between those who call themselves Christians and those who are true disciples of Jesus Christ and live lifestyles of love and obedience.

Daniel was such a man for God. Even though King Nebuchadnezzar had an entire court of magicians, sorcerers, astrologers,

Chaldeans, soothsayers, enchanters, and diviners, Daniel was the only one who could interpret his dream, which was from God as a warning to the king. Even the king knew why Daniel was the only one able to interpret. Daniel 2:10 tells us that the king had a dream no one else could interpret. After Daniel interpreted the dream no one else could, the king said to Daniel (Daniel was also known as Belteshazzar to the king), "Truly your God is the God of gods, the Lord of kings, and a revealer of secrets, since you could reveal this secret" (Daniel 2:47).

The king was so incredibly impacted by the correct interpretation that later he declared it to all peoples, nations, and languages:

> *I thought it good to declare the signs and wonders that the Most High God has worked for me. How great are His signs, and how mighty His wonders! His kingdom is an everlasting kingdom, and His dominion is from generation to generation. I, Nebuchadnezzar, was at rest in my house, and flourishing in my palace. I saw a dream which made me afraid, and the thoughts on my bed and the visions of my head troubled me. Therefore I issued a decree to bring in all the wise men of Babylon before me, that they might make known to me the interpretation of the dream. Then the magicians, the astrologers, the Chaldeans, and the soothsayers came in, and I told them the dream; but they did not make known to me its interpretation. But at last Daniel came before me (his name is Belteshazzar, according to the name of my god; in him is the Spirit of the Holy God), and I told the dream before him, saying: "Belteshazzar, chief of the magicians, because I know that the Spirit of the Holy God is in you, and no secret troubles you, explain to me the visions of my dream that I have seen, and its interpretation" (Daniel 4:2-9).*

Notice, the king was very keenly aware that the Spirit of our Holy God was in Daniel and it clearly set him apart from all the rest. Again, the king says:

> *This dream I, King Nebuchadnezzar, have seen. Now you, Belteshazzar* [Daniel], *declare its interpretation, since all the wise men of my kingdom are not able to make known to me the interpretation; but you are able, for the Spirit of the Holy God is in you* (Daniel 4:18).

We see that the reason Daniel was able to reveal the secret of the message from God in the king's dreams was because he had the Spirit of our Holy God in him. It is the Spirit of God who reveals the secrets of God, and the only way to access them is by receiving the Spirit of God to dwell in you as a believer in Christ Jesus. Take a look at First Corinthians 2:9-12:

> *However, as it is written, "What no eye has seen, what no ear has heard, and what no human mind has conceived"—the things God has prepared for those who love him—these are the things God has revealed to us by His Spirit. The Spirit searches all things, even the deep things of God. For who knows a person's thoughts except their own spirit within them? In the same way no one knows the thoughts of God except the Spirit of God. What we have received is not the spirit of the world, but the Spirit who is from God, so that we may understand what God has freely given us* (NIV).

What this verse basically says is that only those who have the Spirit of God can know the mind of God and be given true understanding from His Holy Spirit. Having the Spirit of God happens when you are spiritually born from above, which means your spirit is born anew with the Holy Spirit from God. That happens the moment you confess your sins, believe that Jesus is the *only* Son of

God (born of a virgin and sinless), confess Jesus as your Lord and Savior, and ask God to fill you with His Holy Spirit.

John 16:13 says, "However, when He, the Spirit of truth [the Holy Spirit dwelling in you], has come, He will guide you into all truth; for He will not speak on His own authority, but whatever He hears He will speak; and He will tell you things to come." *Wow—*it says that when we belong to God and He dwells in us, He will show us what the truth is in any situation, and He will even tell us things that haven't happened yet! Only God knows what we need to know and when we need it. He's not a genie in a bottle or a fortune-teller—rather, He is a compassionate Father who loves to encourage us and give us wisdom.

God reveals secrets to His servants. Again I'll remind you that His servants are those who are truly loving Him and serving Him with their lives and actions, not just those who profess to be Christians. You do not automatically become a Christian just because you go to church or you believe Jesus existed. You *must* live for Him and believe He is the *only* way to live eternally with God.

First Corinthians 4:1 (NIV) says, "This, then, is how you ought to regard us: as servants of Christ and as those entrusted with the mysteries God has revealed." Proverbs 3:32 says, "But His [God's] secret counsel is with the upright." *Upright* means righteous or those whose heart is right with God. Genesis 40:8 says, "And they said to him, 'We each have had a dream, and there is no interpreter of it.' So Joseph said to them, 'Do not interpretations belong to God? Tell them to me, please.'" This verse in Genesis reveals that God is the interpreter of dreams that originate from Him.

If you desire to experience a higher level of spiritual understanding, I urge you to invite the light of God to dwell in your heart, and that light will illuminate your spiritual understanding in a truly supernatural way. If you want more information on what this means, go to Chapter 10, "The Secret Gateway: Invite the Light."

### Love

Clean out your negative filter! I believe one of the most difficult things to help people understand is that God is *loving and kind and good*—and when He speaks, even if what is being said is something we don't really want to hear, it is always said in love. If we simply pursue God, we will be filled with *hope*. More about this is in the following section titled "Fifty Shades of Grace."

### Dream

Now you simply need to dream, then be sensitive to the thoughts you have while you attempt to interpret. Ponder each dream as you wake up and write it down. If you don't have much time to write when you wake up, at least make bullet points that will jog your memory later.

**Keep calm and dream on!**

## FIFTY SHADES OF GRACE

Have you ever noticed how easy it is to believe the worst about yourself? People have a tendency to be overly self-critical and frequently tend to lean in the negative direction with their dream interpretations. I encourage you to err on the side of being positive! If there is something negative that truly needs attention, there will be other confirmations and messages to help you make those adjustments along the way. Just remember…context is *always* the key that unlocks the correct interpretation. Context is in the surrounding situation or details.

I remember one time, while doing a conference on dream interpretation, a woman shared a dream with me, and she was so fearful it meant she was doing something wrong. If I remember correctly, in her dream she was given an old, blue, 1950s pickup truck from her father, and it was all beat up. She had driven down an old, bumpy dirt road and sold it for a $50 profit. Her interpretation of her own dream was filled with fear that she was given a gift by God (the pickup truck) and she didn't take care of it (it was beat up). She thought she neglected it and "sold out" for very little, meaning she felt she might have compromised in some way or put money as a priority.

## Dream Gem: Be kind and renew your mind!

Instantly, I felt the Holy Spirit rise up in me to give her the correct interpretation and encourage her! The interpretation I gave her was that God had given her a gift of revelation. God was the Father in the dream and the gift may have been a spiritual inheritance from her actual earthly family. The old, blue pickup truck was the gift. The color blue can sometimes represent revelation from God in the correct context, and I felt pickup was a word-play meaning she has a gift of picking up on things spiritually—a prophetic gift, a gift of perception or discernment, etc. It was a spiritual gift that had been passed down in her family. Driving down a bumpy dirt road in a beat-up truck revealed that her experience with her prophetic gift of revelation has been a long, hard, bumpy road. The way had not been paved yet (the dirt road), and she had endured a bumpy ride while being verbally beat up over it quite a bit. People had not cherished her and her spiritual gift. The truck not only represented her spiritual ability or gift, but it also revealed how she had been treated. She was the beat-up pickup truck.

At this point in my interpretation, I saw the love and peace of God come over her as she wept bitterly from relief, and her tears were also proof of what she had endured. A pickup truck also often speaks of hard work. I then explained to her that the number 50 was a metaphor and represented incredible freedom or jubilee. When something is mentioned twice, it most often means that it's an established thing, meaning definite. The number 50 was mentioned twice in this dream, with both the truck being from the 1950s and $50 being the selling price. I explained that when she sold the truck to make a profit, what I really felt it meant was that God was commissioning her in her gifting and that she was a *prophet* (wordplay for *profit*), and she again wept in absolute relief. In the dream, she didn't make much money, so that represented she had not sold out for money with her prophetic gifting—the exact opposite of what she feared from her own interpretation.

Do you see how either the negative or positive interpretation could be tangible? The first one came from the enemy chanting failure in her ears and heart. It came through a filter of condemnation. In order to have the positive interpretation, you have to have the heart and mind of God to see the hope, the destiny, and the treasure in the dream. My interpretation was also a confirmation of words other godly and loving people had told her regarding her prophetic gift. God will always confirm His Word to you.

**God always corrects in love with hope.**

It's important to remember that even if God needs to correct us, He will always do it in love and give us a way of hope. Most people do not recognize the subtle difference between condemnation and conviction. Condemnation says, "You're bad! You've done something wrong!" It always makes you feel condemned and never gives you hope. When God corrects, it comes by the way of conviction. Conviction reveals what the issue is, but it always provides a way out or another chance—it always leaves you with hope. This is why it's so important to follow godly dream interpretation.

In the pages ahead, I will continue to give you examples so you can see for yourself how good God is and recognize why His way is the only true way. It's important to steer clear of interpretation models that do not lead you to God and His love.

**Love is the anesthetic for truth.**

## ONE SERIOUS CAUTION

It's incredibly important to remember that God is love and He loves to give people hope. It's His nature. However, while a hopeful interpretation is preferred, there are legitimate warning dreams that we must meticulously be careful not to change the meaning of for the sake of hope. We must speak in love, but making sure we are speaking *truth* in love. Be careful not to replace the truth with fluffy words that water down a warning from God that ultimately is meant to give the dreamer hope of a correct resolution. We also have to remember there are consequences to some of our choices and there isn't always an easy way out. Just as *simple* doesn't necessarily mean "easy," *hopeful* also doesn't mean there is an easy solution or answer.

Many years ago, I felt the Lord gave me a very difficult message to give someone. I pondered it and was concerned it would not be received well. I was nervous about delivering the message and prayed and asked God for help. While praying, I got an image of a needle numbing an area of skin on the back of the hand and felt I heard the Lord say that love is the anesthetic for truth. Hands often represent relationship. God gave me deeper insight into what He was showing me. He gave me understanding that if we have a relationship with someone and we say something with sincere love and the right motive, the love will act as an anesthetic for a difficult message or painful truth. He gave me understanding that if you love people, they will hear what you have to say. They may not always like what you say, but if they know your motive is love, they will receive it in their heart.

Let's be very cautious not to change the meaning of difficult interpretations, but instead saturate them in love *without* sacrificing the truth.

## CINDERELLA: IF THE SHOE FITS

The prince of your dream world wants to help you find your glass slipper! For you guys, there's a beautiful princess who has just the right loafer to make your experience a comfortable one. When interpreting dreams, it's vital to take all things into consideration before coming to a conclusion. There are many hidden things in a dream that will ultimately mean something only to the dreamer. For example, no one would know I have struggled with getting up in the mornings my entire life, and when someone named Dawn is in my dreams, it usually represents "the dawn," as in the morning.

Symbols may also have a specific memory or meaning to the dreamer that no one else will know. For instance, a location in your dream might be a favorite vacation place your family visited as a child. Symbols can have positive meaning for some, while the same symbol for others will carry a negative memory or interpretation. It's important to make a personal assessment of a symbol for yourself when interpreting. It may have a meaning no one else will know; therefore, it may not be listed in any dream dictionary or be a suggestion of a dream interpreter. Remember to only use sources that come from a godly perspective if you want to get a godly interpretation. Also remember that dream dictionaries are to be used only as a source of initial brainstorming and not as a necessarily reliable or final source.

If suggestions for symbol or dream interpretations don't seem to make sense, they probably aren't the right interpretation for a particular person or dream. Keep searching and meditating on the dream elements and symbols until the proverbial shoe fits! Use ancient Scripture, dictionaries, encyclopedias, your life memories, and Internet searches to discover other possibilities.

I personally encourage you to try our *Dreamscapes® Dream Dictionary* app for Apple and Android devices wherever you get apps. Look for our dragonfly icon. The cool thing about our dream dictionary app is that if it doesn't have your symbol listed, you can submit a request and we interpret it and add it to the app! We also have amazing plans to continually add incredible features. Help us get the word out by telling your friends about it. We would appreciate positive reviews, too! There is a way on the app to connect with us if you have issues, comments, or suggestions. You can visit our website for more info: www.gatewaytodreams.com.

## INCEPTION: INTERPRETING *INSIDE OUT!*

Dreams happen in another dimension. Whether it is in our psyche or in the spirit realm, there are things that happen there that don't happen or make sense in the physical or natural realm.

When interpreting, it's important to begin by using the context of the emotions, thoughts, and observations that were happening while you were *inside* the dream. It is very common for people to wake up and begin to mix their natural emotions about something in the dream that did not feel that way while they were dreaming. A common example is being naked in a dream.

If, while *inside* the dream, being naked felt normal, natural, or good, it probably represents something good. Being naked, for instance, can simply mean innocence, vulnerability, or having no hidden motives. When we wake up from dreams like that, however, our natural mind tends to overanalyze and think, *Naked has to be bad,* so we begin to freak out and wonder if we did something wrong. News flash: God created us naked and unashamed. It was only after sin that we became aware and ashamed. And remember, dreams are almost always metaphoric or symbolize something else.

If, however, while *inside* the dream being naked was not a good thing or other immoral things were happening while *inside* the dream, the interpretation may be that too much is being revealed, such as information, motives, etc. Perhaps there is sin and it's being revealed, or maybe it's an "anchor" (explained in the next section) that is "exposing" adultery, pornography, or other issues. Keep in mind, however, most dreams are just us processing our emotions, so a negative-feeling naked dream may also simply reveal we *feel* exposed.

*Important reminder:* Context is always the key—the context that should be used is the context *inside* the dream to begin your interpretation and not your natural knowledge, opinions, fears, etc. that happen upon waking. There is meaning behind your waking emotions, but that subject is covered in more in-depth teachings in our courses, workshops, and future books!

## ANCHORS A WAY!

Even though it goes without saying, there will be literal things in dreams that help indicate what the dream is in reference to in real life. I call these "anchors." Anchors are things in your dreams that are "anchored" to reality to let you know what the dream is about.

I've personally found anchors are usually situations or emotions. Most dreams are simply us processing our emotions; so when approaching an interpretation, take a look at the prevailing emotions in the dream first, and then ask if those emotions are what is currently being dealt with in real life.

For instance, if in the dream there is a lot of fear or confusion, ask yourself if there is fear and confusion in an area of your life right now. If so, that's probably what the dream is about—processing the fear and confusion.

Situations can be things like arguing, dealing with something at work, marital issues, etc. Ask if any of the situations in the dream are happening in real life. If so, the dream may either be helping you process the situation or it may be encouragement, warning, or wisdom about how to handle the situation.

## NO ABSOLUTES! EXCEPT...

As you know by now, when interpreting symbols in dreams, visions, trances, and natural circumstances, be careful to keep the symbol in its proper context to discover the true meaning it has for you personally or for the dreamer you are helping.

There are no absolutes for a symbol! Except...

### God is always good.

God's goodness doesn't always mean easy or pleasant, but it does mean that if you love God, He works all things together for your benefit. Romans 8:28 says, "And we know that all things work together for good to those who love God, to those who are the called according to His purpose."

### Evil symbols are always evil.

Even if they don't look, act, or feel evil. For instance, a witch will *never* be a good symbol. God hates witchcraft, sorcery, magic, fortune-telling, palm reading, curses, spells, etc. Ancient Scriptures reveal witchcraft is an abomination to God, which means vile, shameful, detestable, corrupt, depraved, etc. It means God utterly hates it. *There is no such thing as a good witch.* Many in Wicca will claim there is, but God says there is *not.* There may be witches who do kind things, but that doesn't make being a witch good. Witchcraft is simply any manipulation of the spiritual realm, and manipulating the spirit realm is trying to take control from God. It says in Proverbs 16:25, "There is a way that seems right to a man, but its end is the way of death." We may think we know better than God, but we don't and we have to trust that His ways are higher than our ways and His thoughts are higher than our thoughts. Isaiah 55:9 confirms this truth, "For as the heavens are higher than the earth, so are My ways higher than your ways, and My thoughts than your thoughts." God is good all the time!

Any worship other than that of Jesus Christ is an abomination to God. The Word of God says that everyone will stand before Him without excuse because He has revealed Himself to everyone through everything He has created: "For since the creation of the world His invisible attributes are clearly seen, being understood by the things that are made, even His eternal power and Godhead, so that they are without excuse" (Romans 1:20). Ancient Scripture also says that satan can appear as an angel of light, so we must be careful to examine the symbols and make sure they do not contradict the Word of God or the nature of God.

### Absolutes for symbols are rare.

God speaks to everyone individually, and He speaks to them in a way they can understand. What one thing may mean to you may have a totally different meaning for me. Only you and God know the experiences you've had, the thoughts and opinions you have, the decisions you've made, etc. There are so many things a dream interpreter will never know when interpreting your dreams, and God designed it that way so He could speak to you privately. If none of the possibilities listed under a specific symbol seem to fit, they probably don't. Just ask God what it means, meditate on it, and wait for the answer. The answer may not come right away. Godly meditating is a process and part of our relationship with our Creator. So many times I have sought understanding about a specific symbol in my dream and it came days, weeks, or even years later—and it happened when I least expected it. Many times I received revelation of the meaning while driving down the road pondering the symbol once more, and curiously, I would receive an epiphany and the interpretation would become obvious. I would think to myself, *Wow! That's so obvious, why did it take me so long to get it?* Sometimes what we call "obvious" is not obvious at all, but a secret treasure given to only those who can be entrusted with a jewel from God. He says if you ask for wisdom without doubting, you will be given it, and He reveals treasures to those who seek them. Be a treasure hunter!

### Symbols can have unexpected meanings!

Remember, God says that satan can appear as an angel of light. This means that even though satan is evil, he can make himself look good. This is how he deceives people best. It's easy to detect obvious evil, but what is much harder is to detect evil when it looks good. How can we become sharper at detecting this in our dreams and in real life? The answer is basically twofold: 1) Get to know the Word of God! It will lead you along the wise and ancient path to truth. 2) Guard your heart! I've heard it taught that you can only be deceived if you want to be. I'm still studying to see if this theory is really true, but it is a great marker to take note of.

In other words, we can have a hidden motive on a subconscious level that causes us to listen to or find teaching or advice that we want to hear to justify getting or doing what we want. Even Holy Scripture says:

> *For the time will come when they will not endure sound doctrine, but according to their own desires, because they have itching ears, they will heap up for themselves teachers;*

*and they will turn their ears away from the truth, and be turned aside to fables* (2 Timothy 4:3-4).

Scripture also has so much to say about guarding our hearts and that the heart is the soil (see Phillipians 4:7; Luke 8:15). It also reveals that the soil of our hearts can have many conditions, one of which is hardness of heart—not receiving what God has to say (see Proverbs 28:14). God's Word encourages all believers to listen while we can! It says over and over, "Whoever has ears to hear, let them hear!" (See Matthew 11:15; 13:9,43; Mark 4:9,23; 7:16; Luke 8:8; 14:35.)

## DREAM PATTERNS

One of the many things I've learned the hard way is that everyone has a very specific spiritual gift and also a very specific dream language and pattern. No matter what I teach you in this book or in any of my courses, please keep in mind and pay attention to how you personally dream, how you personally hear from God, and how you are personally gifted spiritually.

What do I mean by this? I remember once talking to a woman on the phone, and she said she dreamt about someone dying. I explained how dreams are mostly symbolic and metaphorical and not to worry. As a precaution, I did encourage her to pray for the person just in case. Three days later, she called me again and said that person had really died. I was utterly dismayed at my poor advice! I had not asked her enough questions about her dream patterns. After talking with her at length, I learned that God often gives her dreams about difficult things to come for people, and we both later learned that God simply wanted her to pray for him to be ready and for comfort for his family—and, thankfully, she had done that.

Another friend of mine often has dreams with people who remind her of other people in her life. For instance, when she has a dream of one friend, it reminds her of another. I came to discover after reviewing many of her dreams that the people in her dreams usually represent someone they remind her of.

Another type of pattern is frequency. As I've already stated about myself, because I'm a seer God tends to use dreams as a primary way to communicate with me, in addition to His Word. I also receive prophetic dreams, which are dreams about the future for something specific, a specific person, or a specific group of people. I often receive dreams for leaders, prophets, pastors, etc., because I am created by God to have influence in that area. Some people rarely remember their dreams, and the lack of dreaming is also a pattern. What this can often reveal is that when these people *do* have a dream, it's important, so they must pay attention! This may be you. So even if it's still just a dream to help you process, the fact you remembered it is to get your attention to deal with something.

Depending on your heart for issues, people, or certain areas in your life that matter to you, you may also see patterns of dreams for those specific things. In other words, if you have a marriage ministry or are a counselor, you may get dreams for specific marriages, etc.

The caution with dreaming about things you know is that it's often a metaphor, using something you understand to explain something you don't. As I've previously mentioned, one of the most common occurrences is when people dream of work. They tell me, "I dream about my work because I work all the time!" In reality, because God uses things we understand as examples to explain things we may not understand, I have found that work is usually a metaphor to help them understand something else going on in their lives that may take some *hard work*. The work dreams are often used as a parable or story of sorts so they can comprehend the comparison. Even dreams from our own conscience or soul draw parallels to help us cope or work through other things that are going on.

It's as if God or your very soul is saying, "You know how when you're at work and this happens...well, it also applies to this other area of your life!" That way you can have an "aha" moment because you now have understanding.

## REGARDING DREAM DICTIONARIES

There are several dream dictionaries available on the market, both Christian and non-Christian. All can occasionally be correct or at least get you close to a correct interpretation from time to time by applying simple common sense for common symbols. But there are two very important issues concerning these dictionaries that I must bring to your attention, which I feel are vital if you are to have a successful dream journey.

### 1. The Issue with Non-Christian Dream Dictionaries

The primary issue with non-Christian dream dictionaries is the authors do not have God's perspective. Not everything spiritual is godly. The Bible says the invisible realm is more real than the visible one. The bottom line is that even if it's spiritual, if it doesn't come *from* God, it will not lead you *to* God. Ancient Scriptures reveal that if you do not have the Spirit of God, being born from above by accepting Jesus Christ as your Lord and Savior, then you will not be filled with His Holy Spirit and you cannot understand the mind of God.

I went to the library one day and thumbed through several non-Christian dream dictionaries and was overwhelmed with sadness as I read page after page of doom and gloom—many symbols being the exact opposite of what God says. Again, if it does not come *from* God, it will not lead you *to* God.

## 2. The Issue with Christian Dream Dictionaries

Context is more important to God than the symbol itself, and not everything is in the Bible.

When I first discovered dreams had meaning, I immediately located a Christian book on dreams, and it had a small dictionary in it. I remember having tons of dreams with beautiful green, thick grass. I was excited to see what it meant and quickly turned to the page that had the symbol for grass. I remember the fear that came over me as I read that it meant "flesh," suggesting that it was something carnal or in my own desires and will, instead of spiritual and God's desires and will. For two entire years I was tormented that I must be doing something wrong. I later learned grass can also mean the Word of God or growth in areas of my life. I was so relieved that I began to cry as I felt condemnation fall off me and God's hope fill my heart that my dreams were good and not evil.

What I discovered with most Christian dream dictionaries is that their authors' intentions are good, but they can lack balance. Some dictionaries only list things that are in the Bible and neglect the fact that God can still use symbols of today to speak to us because He's a very personal God. For instance, guns are not in the Bible, but it doesn't keep God from using them as a symbol in your dreams. I had a dream with a gun in it one time, and while I was in the dream the Holy Spirit told me that guns often mean people who are using hurtful words or "shooting off at the mouth." It represented harmful words intended to destroy people. He then showed me the destruction it caused someone, and then the Holy Spirit revealed to me, while I was still in the dream, that people will give an account when they stand before God for every idle word they speak. Matthew 12:36 says, "But I say to you that for every idle word men may speak, they will give account of it in the day of judgment."

Another example would be dogs. I have found dogs in Scripture to always have a negative meaning. I discovered the reason was because in that day and culture dogs were not pets. Instead, they roamed the streets and ate anything around. In Scripture, dogs represent people who return to their evil ways, people who are contentious, backbiters, etc. Just because dogs were a negative symbol in Scripture doesn't mean they are always a negative symbol in dreams. For instance, if a dog represents loyalty and "man's best friend" to you, God can use it in your dreams to represent a best friend who is loyal. It may also be a reflection of you personally, as dreams are often reflecting characteristics of the dreamer.

What I've learned over and over is that God will use the things you understand to explain the things you don't. He loves to speak to you in your language, and He will use things that have meaning to you personally. Remember, Jesus only used parables to speak to the crowds, and He used symbols and circumstances people could understand at the time.

The issue is always context, context, context! The primary issue when interpreting symbols is to first check the Word of God to see what examples God gives and, more importantly, why and what is the context of the symbol. Context is the situation that surrounds the symbol. Throughout Scripture you can see the same symbol represented in both a positive context and a negative context. There are also some symbols that have several meanings in Scripture based on the context in which they are used. In addition to Scripture, it's important to take into consideration personal references, wordplays, riddles, idioms, etc.

Let's look at *lion* as an example. Some meanings of *lion* in Scripture:

- Jesus, strong and powerful! See Isaiah 31:4 (the Lord); Revelation 5:5 refers to Jesus.

- God's judgment or power. See Hosea 5:14; 11:10; First Kings 13:26; Amos 3:7-8.

- To be fearless, courageous, and bold. See Proverbs 30:30; 28:1.

- Strong. See Judges 14:18; Second Samuel 1:23.

- Valiant. See Second Samuel 17:10.

- Vicious or fierce. See Psalm 7:2; 22:13; 57:4; First Kings 13:26; Job 4:10; 10:16; 28:8.

- Ruthless people who have secret, evil motives. See Psalm 10:9; 17:12; Lamentations 3:10; Ezekiel 22:25.

- The enemy, satan, trying to intimidate and devour people. See First Peter 5:8.

Other possible interpretations of lion:

- Pride, because a group of lions is called a pride. Pride is also the reason satan fell from Heaven and he is compared to a lion (see First Peter 5:8).

- Lion may be a wordplay for telling falsehoods, *lying* (*lyin'*).

How lion may be interpreted more personally:

- If lions remind you of Africa, it may reveal something about Africa.

- If you know people with the last name Lyon, it may be a hint it involves them or is about them.

- It may reveal a sports team with the name Lions, such as the Detroit Lions.

- It may indicate a company with the name Lion in it, such as Thai Lion Air, Lions Pictures, or Food Lion grocery stores.

- It may be a hidden key to a company or entity that has a lion for a symbol, icon, or logo, such as MGM, Red Lion Hotels, Peugeot, ING Bank, or the national emblem of Great Britain.

Consider dictionary meanings for a symbol. The following are a few that may come into consideration for interpreting a dream:

- A man of great strength.

- "A person of great importance, influence, charm, etc., who is much admired as a celebrity: 'a literary lion.'"[1]

- "A member of any one of the internationally affiliated service clubs (International Association of Lions Clubs)."[2]

- The constellation Leo. (God created the constellations, not the new age. He has a different meaning than they do!) The Leo constellation may be a reference to Jesus.

Lion idioms:

- "*Beard the lion in its den* means to confront or attack someone, especially a powerful or feared person, in that person's own familiar surroundings."[3]

- "*Twist the lion's tail* means to tax the patience of or provoke a person, group, nation, or government, especially that of Great Britain."[4]

It's vitally important to consider all that's going on in the dream concerning the lion. For instance, the fact that there's a lion in the dream may not be as important as what the lion is doing or the description of the lion. For example, consider:

- What is the lion doing? Is he sleeping, prowling, roaring, or eating? Is the lion playing with cubs or protecting something?

- What's the condition or description of the lion? Is the lion hungry or angry? Is his mane tangled? Is the lion a male or female?

## Be Mindful Not to Have Absolutes!

Another area where I frequently see error with Christian dream interpretation and the use of dream dictionaries is what we've already discussed—having absolutes. One example is the interpretation for *car*. Almost every Christian I've encountered who interprets a car in their dream will say it represents ministry because that's what they've been taught. This is a dangerous assumption. The first reason it may not represent ministry is because not everyone is called to ministry, especially non-Christians, so why would a car always represent ministry? Yes, we are all called to minister, but we are not all called to ministry. I, personally, have found cars to represent numerous things, such as your own personal ambition or motives, your marriage, your job, your relationships with others, and many other things. It's also important to take into consideration the context, the condition of the car, the type, size, style, model, etc. It may not be as much about the fact that it's a car as it may be about the condition or description of the car. For instance, are the tires flat? Perhaps it reveals feeling "tired" or "deflated." Is it rusty? Perhaps you're feeling "rusty" at something or maybe a relationship is being neglected, needs to be protected, etc.

## Balance and Context Are the Keys!

I hope you see how important it is to take everything into consideration and be mindful to stay balanced! Keep these issues in mind when you are delving into dream dictionaries. Better yet, please consider using the dream interpretation guides discussed in the remainder of this book. They are based on intensive Bible study, extensive personal experience, and Holy Spirit-inspired revelations.

## JEDI DREAM TIPS:

- Use the Bible, dictionaries, encyclopedias, the Internet, your life's memories, etc. to research and brainstorm for possible symbol meanings.

- Get our *Dreamscapes®* *Dream* *Dictionary* app for phones and tablets!

- Context is ALWAYS the key to a correct interpretation.

- Most dreams are us simply processing our emotions.

- Avoid absolutes.

- Use extreme caution with dream dictionaries and don't become dependent on them.

## ENDNOTES

1.  *Dictionary.com*, s.v. "Lion," accessed January 20, 2015, http://dictionary.reference.com.

2.  Ibid.

3.  Ibid.

4.  Ibid.

# Chapter 9

# LET'S GET STARTED! SIMPLIFYING DREAM INTERPRETATION

## WHAT'S YOUR CUP OF T.E.A.?
## 3 SIMPLE STEPS TO UNDERSTANDING YOUR DREAMS

There are dozens, if not hundreds of ways to approach dream interpretation, and depending on your learning style some will be much more effective for you than others. I teach various different models in-depth at our courses, workshops, and seminars. After many years of just asking God a million questions, searching ancient Scripture and meditating on my dreams, I realized dream interpretation can usually be reduced to a simple three-step approach. I call it having a cup of T.E.A. This cup of T.E.A. is a delicate blend of:

- **T** = Titles or Turning Points
- **E** = Emotions
- **A** = Actions

## GETTING STARTED

Just like drinking a cup of hot tea, I encourage you to approach dream interpretation by sipping, not gulping! Just keep it simple and move through the process one sip at a time. As you embark on your dream interpretation journey, remember to return to the simplicitTEA of this model if interpreting begins to feel too heavy. Now let's explore these three simple steps more closely.

### T = Title or Turning Point

"T" in T.E.A. stands for Title or Turning Point (a turning point can also be a climax of a story). One of the easiest ways to title your dreams is to figure out what the climax or turning point in the dream is. This is usually what the dream is ultimately about. The climax is the ultimate peak or summit of the storyline. Think of a dream as a book or movie and ask yourself, *When does my dream come to its ultimate peak?*

One way you can try to find the climax of the dream is to chart the dream with a triangle. Begin by drawing a triangle. At the bottom left tip, write the beginning actions of the story. Along the left side going up, write the rising action. The top of the triangle is the climax or turning point. Along the right side going down, write the falling action where the story settles down. The bottom right tip is the ending.

Many times, whatever is written as the climax of the dream is the best title for the dream and it gives you a clue as to what the dream is about. The fable of "Little Red Riding Hood" is used for an example. It is a children's story you can find in any bookstore or on the Internet. You may want to familiarize yourself with it in order to understand the example.

Every story or dream has:

1.  A beginning action.

2.  A rising action or incline.

3.  A turning point or climax.

4.  Most have a falling action or decline.

5.  An ending.

See the following chart as an example:

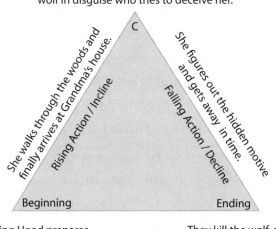

Little Red Riding Hood encounters a wolf in disguise who tries to deceive her.

C

She walks through the woods and finally arrives at Grandma's house.

Rising Action / Incline

She figures out the hidden motive and gets away in time.

Falling Action / Decline

Beginning

Ending

Little Red Riding Hood prepares to go to Grandma's house.

They kill the wolf, set Grandma free, and live happily ever after.

Looking at the climax (C) or turning point at the top, we could reword it a bit and title the dream, "Deceived by a Wolf," "Encountering a Wolf in Disguise," or "Little Red Riding Hood Deceived by a Wolf in Disguise." Now, when you interpret the symbols for the fable Little Red Riding Hood, you'll understand what the dream is about.

The following are some possible interpretations for the symbols if this had been an actual dream (keeping in mind that because grandmas can sometimes be literal, though very rare, it may possibly be referring to an actual person).

*Little Red Riding Hood* = Someone who is walking in wisdom, anointing, or power and under the authority of the blood of Jesus (the color red can mean these things). Her age may represent a level of maturity or perhaps her being young simply restates the fact that she represents someone who is wise beyond his or her years.

*The Wolf* = May represent a specific person with ulterior motives, such as the saying, "A wolf in sheep's clothing." It may also be much more abstract representing a deceptive belief or teaching, for example.

*Grandma* = She may represent a generational issue, such as wrong beliefs, addictions, or issues in a family that keep happening. Grandma could also simply represent something "old" such as teachings or ways of thinking. It may also represent an awesome spiritual inheritance because grandparents sometimes leave an inheritance to their children and grandchildren.

*Abduction* = Taken captive by false teaching that keeps people from living in freedom and also puts others at risk. It may also indicate that although Grandma is nice, she was naïve and caught off guard. This would be giving us insight or instruction to pay attention and not be naïve—the lesson would be to be careful, to not blindly trust every teaching or situation.

*The Wolf in Disguise Trying to Kill Everyone* = The enemy, who is satan, wanting everyone to believe lies so he can kill, steal, and destroy them. The enemy does not want people to experience freedom. It may also represent a person who is being controlled by the enemy and has ulterior motives. It may even be someone who claims to be a Christian but is not—"Beware of wolves in sheep's clothing" (see Jesus's words in Matthew 7:15).

*Killing the Wolf* = Taking every thought captive and making sure it agrees with the Word of God. Destroying the works of the enemy and setting the captives free! It may also reveal someone who needs to be removed from a situation because the person has ulterior motives and intends harm.

## When the Story Ends at the Climax

Some dreams or stories end at the climax. Like many stories end in cliff-hangers, the reason a dream may not have a decline or closure may be because the dream reveals there is not yet a definite outcome. If a dream does not have an ending, it often indicates that prayer and choices may alter the outcome. Another reason a dream may end abruptly at the climax is because the dream may be about something in your life you're currently in the midst of and it has not yet ended.

### Simply title each climax or turning point.

Also note that some stories have multiple rises and falls, just as some dreams have multiple scenes or issues going on one after another. In that case, simply title *each* climax or turning point. A dream may be about multiple issues all at the same time or the multiple climaxes show many different ways of revealing the same issue.

## Identifying Situations, Issues, and Conditions to Help You Title Dreams

After studying thousands of dreams, I have found that they are usually about us processing our emotions or dealing with situations and issues in life. When I began to use the titling approach, I found that one of the easiest ways to title was to include the emotions and to pinpoint the situation, issue, or problem of the dream.

If we use the Little Red Riding Hood example as though it were a dream, we would discover that some of the situations, issues, or problems would be deception, abduction, and an attack. If we used any of these words in our title, we would discover that's exactly what the dream was about and know what to be aware of, what to pray about, or how to respond.

Conditions are usually adjectives or descriptive words. The amazing aspects of these words are that they often describe your emotions and issues. For instance, if something is rusty, you may be feeling that way about something, such as feeling rusty about teaching, etc. Bent out of shape is another description. What does it make you think of? To be "bent out of shape" is an American saying that means to get angry. You will find there are more than 8,000 figures of speech in the Bible, and they are very common ways God communicates not only in Scripture, but also in your dreams. As another example, if there is something in the dream that has been abandoned, then ask yourself if there is anything in your life that you've perhaps neglected or abandoned, such as a project, a relationship, someone's physical condition, etc. Condition or describing words are very helpful in dream interpretation and can often lead you right to the anchor that reveals what's going on in your life!

### E = Emotions

The "E" in T.E.A. stands for Emotions. Whenever giving two or three titles to your dream, I encourage people to include one of the primary emotions of the dream in at least one of the titles. Most dreams are about us processing things in our lives, and those "things" are usually emotions or situations.

If we again use Little Red Riding Hood as an example, perhaps one of the titles would be, "Afraid of the Wolf" or "Relieved Grandma is Alive" or "Confused Why Grandma Is Acting so Strange." You can see the emotions are fear, relief, and confusion. The first thing to ask yourself, because most dreams are about us processing our emotions, is *Am I experiencing any of these emotions anywhere in my real life right now?* Usually, the answer is a resounding, *"Yes!"* If so, then you can reexamine the dream and see if it makes sense in the context of what's going on in your real waking life. If the answer is "No," then it may reveal something is on the horizon to get prepared for by praying and being alert.

## A = Actions

The "A" in T.E.A. stands for Actions. Actions are the verbs in the dream or what is happening. These can come in past, present, or future tense. Some examples:

- Speak, speaking, spoke

- Walk, walking, walked

- Argue, arguing, argued

- Build, building, built

I have found that the action in the dream is often the issue at hand in real life or at least an effective title. It usually describes something you're processing, have encountered recently or currently, or it may be things to come if it doesn't seem to fit in the past or present.

If the context is right, sometimes the action can be hidden instruction of what you are supposed to do in response to the dream. For instance, God revealed to me that when I am *sharing* a dream I had with someone *while I am inside of a dream* that is an instruction from God to actually *share* the dream with the person in real life.In this case, sharing and interpreting are the actions.

In the example of Little Red Riding Hood, perhaps her *recognizing* something isn't right with Grandma (who is really the wolf), may represent that the dreamer *recognizes* something that just isn't right with someone or something they've recently encountered in their waking life, such as a person with ulterior motives. The action in this case would be "recognizing."

## HIDDEN PICTURES AND SPIRITUAL SCAVENGER HUNTS!

Sitting in the doctor's or dentist's office as a child, I would immediately gravitate to the children's magazine, *Highlights*. Most of you probably know exactly what I'm talking about and are smiling right now! I would skip past all the children's stories and go right to the "Hidden Pictures" page where the hunt began to see how many hidden objects I could find and circle! If you haven't experienced this fabulous children's magazine, the "Hidden Pictures" page was a picture with a list next to it of hidden objects to find and circle.

Dreams are very much like hidden pictures or spiritual scavenger hunts! They don't always make sense right away, and you have to look for all the hidden objects or symbols first and then allow the Holy Spirit to put the pieces of the puzzle together—and it's so much *fun!*

I remember when I first began my dream interpretation adventure. I approached it the way I approached studying the Bible—interpreting it line upon line and precept upon precept, being careful to follow the subject in context. When I first began dream interpretation, I would read my dream line by line and try to interpret it in the order that I wrote it out. After several years, I finally realized that interpreting dreams is entirely different and very subjective.

I remember laughing when God gave me a dream to explain how a dream interpretation comes together! Those who know me know that I *love* books! I have an extensive library, and I organize my books by topic first and then by height so it looks nice and neat.

In the dream, I was in my office and I had a boss who was asking me to arrange the books on the bookshelves. My boss kept telling me to put them in alphabetical order. I resisted and said, "No! If we do it that way, it will look very messy and random." He insisted I put them in alphabetical order from A to Z. Once again, I resisted and showed him the difference by making them nice and neat by height from left to right. He loved how I put it together so it looked good, and he finally agreed that was how we should do it.

When I awoke from the dream, the title I gave my dream was, "It's better to organize how it looks nicest." I began laughing as I felt God show me how dream interpretation is the same way. You have to find all the hidden things first and then let the Holy Spirit *highlight* what is important and put it in the order that is the *nicest*—because God is an encourager! *Neat*, huh? I was so stuck on a specific way and order to interpret, and God used this dream to show me how to relax and allow Him to author the interpretations.

It's like a great recipe that has all the ingredients—sometimes there is an order for when each ingredient is added, and sometimes it doesn't matter. Each dream recipe is different, and it's the Holy Spirit's job to help lead you into all truth. Unlike interpreting Scripture, where you *must* interpret in order and be careful to stay very *objective*, dream interpretation is *subjective* and is not necessarily interpreted in the order the dream occurs.

## THE DREAM WHISPERER: BECOMING A DREAM INVESTIGATOR

Questions are the "w" and the "h" in the word *whisper*! They are the *who, what, where, when, why,* and the *how* to help you become an effective dream investigator. Here's an acronym to help you remember a handful of things that will help you both title your dreams and interpret them. The acronym is QUESTIONS, which will help you discover hidden treasures in your dreams.

Effective titles are usually one or more of the following:

- **Q**—Questions to be resolved

- **U**—Unique symbols

- **E**—Emotions
- **S** – Summations
- **T**—Turning point(s) or the climax
- **I**—Inside observations (inside the dream)
- **O**—Outside observations (upon wakening)
- **N**—Notable words or sentences
- **S**—Situations, actions, or issues

These are simply nine approaches that may help you title dreams quicker and more effectively. Find one or two that make the most sense to you. You do not need to apply every approach. Everyone learns differently based on how God created them, so there is no right or wrong way—just different ways to apply the same information. The Little Red Riding Hood fable is used in the following examples, so you may once again want to familiarize yourself with the fable in order to understand. Let's take a look at each letter in the acronym, QUESTIONS.

## Q = Questions to Ask or Be Resolved

Have you ever watched the game show on television called *Jeopardy*? The contestants are given the answer to a topic and their reply is the question that is being answered. Asking questions will lead to answers that resolve problems. Titling this way will often lead you to what your response to the dream should be. The following are some questions that may need a resolution in Little Red Riding Hood:

1. Why are Grandma's eyes, ears, nose, and teeth so big?
2. Why is Grandma acting strange?
3. Where is Grandma?
4. How did the wolf get in here?

Answering questions gives you very accurate titles that will reveal specific insight into the meaning of the dream.

Examples of questions and corresponding titles follow:

- *Question:* Why are Grandma's eyes, ears, nose, and teeth so big?

  *Titles:* Grandma Is Not Herself; Grandma Has Big Eyes, Ears, Nose, and Teeth; What's Wrong with Grandma?

- *Question:* Why is Grandma acting strange?

  *Titles:* Grandma Is Acting Strange; You're Not Grandma!; Suspicious Person

- *Question:* Where is Grandma?

  *Titles:* This Is Not Grandma; I Need to Find Grandma; I Need to Find Out Who This Really Is

- *Question:* How did the wolf get in here?

  *Titles:* Find Out How the Wolf Got In; Kill the Wolf; Deception Discovered!

Answering the five "Ws" and the "H" questions will help you summarize the dream and also assist you in discovering effective titles. Examples:

- *Who* = Little Red Riding Hood, Grandma, the wolf

- *What* = Encountered a wolf, abduction, deception

- *Where* = Grandma's house

- *When* = On the visit (sometimes it will be a specific time, season, month, etc.)

- *Why* = The wolf had ulterior motives, Grandma was abducted, Little Red Riding Hood thought it was Grandma

- *How* = The wolf abducted Grandma and disguised himself as her, Little Red Riding Hood begins to notice things are not right

*Title examples* in this case would be much like newspaper headlines. Try to keep them as brief as possible to simply convey the main issue or headline.

- A Wolf Abducts Grandma

- Wolf Dead after Discovered Deception

- Lesson in Paying Attention to Details

- Red Riding Hood Discovers Wolf

- Beware of Wolves!

- Wolf Uses Disguise to Deceive and Attempts to Devour Girl

- Breaking and Entering

For a full interpretation, you would go back and summarize all the information into one complete thought, just as a newspaper reporter does in the first paragraph of a news article, highlighting just the main facts first and then expounding later in the remainder of the article. We also call this the *summation*, which is an "S" in the QUESTIONS acronym.

*Example Summation:* While on her visit to Grandma's house, Little Red Riding Hood encountered a wolf who abducted her grandmother and tried to eat her. The wolf was killed and Grandma was set free and they are much more careful not to be so naïve.

Dream titles may often be metaphoric or symbolic themselves and require further interpretation. For instance, if Little Red Riding Hood were a dream and you titled it instead, "Beware of the Wolf," you would then have to interpret what a wolf would represent. Always take at least a glance at what every symbol would represent if it were a metaphor or symbolic. For example, people in dreams are rarely themselves, but if you don't take the time to think metaphorically, you may think the dream is really about them. In this case, you may think the dream is about Grandma or Little Red Riding Hood, but in reality it may simply be about the issue of deception and being careful.

### U = Unique Symbols

Things happen in dreams that simply do not happen in the natural, which is why I love them so much! One time I had a dream and there was a pond or a small pool of water, and I saw the cutest animal swimming in it. The animal looked like a beaver or an otter, but I kept calling it an ott. Even while I was in the dream I kept saying, "Ott. Ott? What is an ott?" I would declare! This adorable little animal was jumping and playing in the water and having so much fun! I looked up the word *ott* and it was an acronym meaning "over the top." The name of my nonprofit organization is "Above & Beyond!" (Or "over the top!") After further investigation on the Internet, I also found that Ott is a brand of light, created by Dr. John Nash Ott. It's a type of indoor lighting that is more natural and replicates natural light. One of the descriptions for their type of light is that you can see the details more clearly and the colors are true to life. Ott light is also a full-spectrum light. Spectrum, when interpreted, represents the rainbow, which also represents God's promises. God revealed to me that I was the ott, and I was reflecting His light, which is His truth, in a fun way by explaining to people the details and making them clearer and easier to understand.

The Ott light also reduces eye strain, and I felt God say that my way of interpreting is easier and people don't have to strain as much! Isn't that amazing how God will use something we have no previous knowledge or frame of reference for? If we take the time to unearth the buried treasure, we will find incredible dream gems and grow in our relationship with God! Another crazy thing that happened later on was when I was in a store and saw a light called OttLite and God brought that dream back to my remembrance. I love how fun God is! This dream is also a great example of how your dreams can be allegories.

## E = Emotions

See the T.E.A. section on emotions.

## S = Summations

Quick, concise, one-line headlines. We've already discussed summations; however, to recap, they are reporter-like headlines for newspapers. They summarize what's going on in the dream in one or two concise sentences, covering all the main facts or issues. This will usually give you a precise interpretation for the dream!

## T = Turning Point or Climax

See T.E.A. section at the beginning of this chapter.

## I = Inside Observations (while inside the dream)

One of the most important things you can do when interpreting dreams is to remember to interpret inside out as we've already discussed. When interpreting your dream, it's important to keep the emotions you had while you were *inside* the dream and be careful not to confuse the emotions after you woke up as part of your interpretation. There is a place for waking emotions and thoughts, but stay in the context of the dream initially.

## O = Outside Observations (upon awakening)

We go much more in-depth on this issue in our dream interpretation courses listed on our website; however, let me just make a few quick observations about this issue for your reference now. Outside observations are those things you think and feel after you wake up from the dream. It's important to take notice of what your first thoughts and impressions are when you awake after a dream and perhaps write them down for reference, noting that they happened after you woke up.

Immediate thoughts and feelings upon waking won't always be correct, but they are very important and can play a vital role in interpretation. Some of the following questions or observations you have when you first wake up might be things such as: Did you think of a person or situation or an issue when you first woke up? Did you think of a Bible verse? What was the time on the clock? Often, the time on the clock can represent a Bible chapter and verse. Outside observations usually are not necessary, but they do add an entirely new dimension and insight and can sometimes be the key to finding the hidden treasures in your dreams.

## N = Notable Words or Sentences

Notable words and sentences can be several things. Sometimes they are words that stick out like a sore thumb and catch your attention—usually words you don't normally use. Another pattern to look for are words that are repeated over and over throughout the dream as you write it down. This is common when studying the Bible, too. You will find themes in both Scripture and in your dreams as you take note of a word, concept, or theme that is repeated over and over. One of the most intriguing patterns I have discovered is when you're thinking of one word as you're writing your dream down, but you end up writing down an entirely different word that means the same thing. When this happens pay close attention! That is the Holy Spirit trying to get your attention. As a reminder to you, God once told me in a dream that one word will unlock the entire dream.

**One word will unlock the entire dream.**

### S = Situations, Actions, or Issues (resolved or not)

Dreams will often contain issues that either get resolved or need to be resolved. Issues can be good, bad, or indifferent, and they consist of things like conflicts, problems that arise, encounters that happen, choices, etc.

If we stay with the Little Red Riding Hood example and title some of the issues happening, they could include the following:

- "Preparing to Go to Grandma's House"

- "Grandma Is Acting Strange"

- "What I Thought Was Grandma Was Really a Wolf"

- "Where Is Grandma?"

- "Encountering a Deceptive Wolf," etc.

## PUZZLED

Are you still puzzled about the meaning of your dreams? Let's take yet another look at how to interpret dreams. Dream interpretation can be just like putting a puzzle together. Each dream puzzle is different and will have different levels of difficulty or ease, and each one will have its own number of pieces. The strategy for dream interpretation is very much the same as that of putting a puzzle together.

### *Find the Corner Pieces First!*

The corner pieces of a puzzle are the easiest to find, and that's where most people begin. The dream interpretation process is the same! The first thing you do is find the corner pieces of the dream, which are those things that are the most obvious or easiest to understand. Doing this will help you put the other pieces of your dream puzzle together faster.

What are the corner pieces? The four corner pieces of a dream are usually:

1.   The title of the dream as if it were a book, movie, or song.

2.   The main emotion(s) in the dream.

3.   The main issues or themes throughout the dream.

4.   Anything in the dream that is going on in real life. I call these dream anchors. They anchor the dream to reality.

### *Next, the Edge Pieces!*

The edge pieces of a puzzle all have a straight or flat side, so it's the next easiest thing to locate out of the pile of puzzle pieces. There are many more edge pieces than corner pieces. Edge pieces in a dream are the next obvious things that create the context of the dream—the setting, themes, turning point, questions, repetitive or unique words, symbols, and observations. These things tell you which direction to go with your interpretation and what it probably relates to.

The edge pieces are the:

1.   Setting—the location where the dream takes place and the mood.

2.   Themes—main emotions, issues, or problems.

3.   Turning Point—when or how does the dream change direction? (The turning point can also be a corner piece.)

Let's look more closely at some of the edge pieces.

### Setting

Settings are usually where a dream takes place inside the dream. For instance, it could be the Wild West, outer space, your parent's house, your workplace, the past, present, or future, etc.

### Themes

Themes are the main topic, the unifying or dominant emotion, issue, or problem, etc. For instance, is the main topic a beautiful wedding or doing something at work? Is there a theme of anger, fear, or excitement? Is there a specific problem to be solved like trying to find something or needing to accomplish something? Are there any issues that stand out, like people fighting in the dream or being lost in the woods, etc.?

### Turning Point

Titling your turning point is a quick way to discover what the dream is probably about. Turning points are usually the climax of the dream story. There can be several climaxes in a dream, just as there are in movies and books, so the more titles, the better! Remember, these can also be corner pieces—a major piece to solving the dream puzzle.

### *The Inside Pieces*

The main thing to remember about inside pieces of the dream puzzle is that, just like when you put a real puzzle together, sometimes you have to keep turning the piece until it fits somewhere. There will be things you interpret in your dream that you think fit, only to find out later they don't quite fit where or how you thought they did. Just remain teachable as you navigate your way waist-high through your dreams. It can get deep at times, and when it does, remember to go back to the edge pieces and oversimplify it and keep it in context!

Here are some inside pieces to work on:

1. The questions—who, what, where, when, why, and how.

2. Repetitive words or symbols.

3. Unique words or symbols.

4. Thoughts and observations.

Let's dive into the inside pieces.

**The Questions**

Asking questions will reveal many pieces to your puzzle! They are the typical five Ws and the H we have already discussed in "The Dream Whisperer: Becoming a Dream Investigator" section above.

- *Who*: Who is in the dream and what might they symbolize to you? (See "People" in Chapter 11, "How to Interpret 21 Symbolic Categories.")

- *What*: What's going on, what do you feel, what are you observing, what can be or should be done about things, etc.?

- *Where*: Where is the dream located, where are you going or where are you coming from, where did you put something, etc.?

- *When*: When did something change in the dream, when did you have the dream, etc.? *When* can also reveal a period of time the dream occurred in, such as past, present, or future.

- *Why*: Are there clues in the dream that reveal why something happened? Why do you think you felt the way you did in the dream; why were other people doing, saying, or feeling the way they were, etc.?

- *How*: How was something created, resolved, instigated, etc.? How should issues in the dream have been handled instead; were there instructions how to accomplish something, etc.?

## Repetitive Words or Symbols

Finding repetitive words in your dream can be incredibly insightful! This is difficult to find unless you write your dreams down. Many times we won't think about what words we would choose to describe something unless we write about it. Writing your dreams down is incredibly important, and you will discover hidden insights as you do! One of the treasures is the wording you end up using as you write things down. This is a hidden key to dream interpretation. *Prime examples of repetitive words are words that describe the emotions, actions, or objects in the dream.*

*Emotions:* Many times when I'm interpreting a dream for someone and I keep hearing them say words like, "Then I was scared, I was afraid, there was intense fear," etc., I know the dream is most likely about them processing their fear of something specific. Other details of the dream will reveal the *what*, but even if you have a difficult time finding what they are afraid of in the dream, you can ask them, "Is there anything right now you are afraid of?" and you will often discover there is something they're processing in real life they're afraid of, such as being afraid of not pleasing someone or afraid they will not accomplish what they are supposed to, etc.

*Actions* are those things that are happening in the dream. For instance, is something being worked on, are you going somewhere, are there trees being cut down, etc.? Many times you will see something in dreams that keeps happening over and over, and it's most likely what the dream is about in real life. Whatever is happening may be symbolic, so there may need to be some interpretation in order to understand it. If we were to interpret what trees mean, for instance, symbolically they most often represent people. Therefore, the example of cutting down trees repetitively in a dream may be indicating that people are being "cut down" (slandered or judged).

*Objects or symbols:* When we speak of objects and/or symbols that are repetitive, note that it can happen in two different ways. One way is that the object or symbol repetitively appears in the same dream. The other way is that you have lots of different dreams with the same symbol. *Repetitive words are most often emotions, actions, and objects.*

## Unique Words or Symbols

In contrast to repetitive words, there are *unique* words or symbols. These are usually words you typically wouldn't use or even things that don't actually exist in real life. Another thing that often happens when you write your dreams down is you will find you are thinking one word, but instead write down a different word. These are Holy Spirit "aha" moments. Pay close attention when that happens! It's usually very strategic and insightful. For example, God once revealed to me in a dream that one word can unlock the entire dream. I believe that to also be true of Scripture.

## Thoughts and Observations

After sifting through thousands of dreams—mine and others'—I've discovered one of the most important parts to dream interpretation is asking questions about the thoughts and observations the dreamer had while he or she was inside the dream. Many times there is no way to get an accurate interpretation without having this knowledge. Many thoughts and observations are hidden knowledge in the dreamer's heart and mind that isn't revealed unless specifically asked. For example, as I allude to in other places throughout this book, sometimes the specific symbol is not as important as the condition of it or the description of it, such as size, color, etc. For instance, maybe there was a car in a dream. If the entire car was rusty (the condition of the car), that fact would be more important to a correct interpretation than the fact it was a car.

Another example are observations that the dreamer usually neglects to write down, like specifics that have meaning to you in real life or subtle observations, such as if something was missing or if you had thoughts while inside the dream that seemed fleeting or irrelevant to you at the time. As you recall a dream, you may mention little things like, "I remember thinking, *Why is that chair over there?*" etc. If you neglect to ask yourself about what you were thinking and observing inside the dream, you will have no idea how to lean with the interpretation—many times thoughts and observations are important keys that unlock your dreams.

## HOLLYWEIRD: WHAT'S YOUR DREAM RATED?

Almost everyone says their dreams are weird and dismiss them because of that. Dreams are meant to be weird because of their symbolic nature. Here's a quick and general rule of thumb to give you an easy starting point for understanding the basics of your dreams—if the dream was a movie, what would it be rated?

### G - Good

G dreams are usually amazing and include encounters, visitations, angels, joy, love, purity, etc. These dreams are *good* or *God-dreams*. They can also include things like cartoons, which usually represent our *character* or integrity.

## PG

As in real life, PG stands for some parental guidance advised. PG in dreams usually stands for *pretty good*, though there may be a thing or two in the dream that felt negative, wrong, or distasteful. Most dreams fall into this rating or category. These are usually dreams that are normal emotional processing dreams.

## PG-13

I call these dreams average dreams and may contain some rebellion in them. The number 13 often, though not always, represents rebellion in Scripture. Rebellion in dreams can appear as cursing, smoking—especially marijuana—stealing, etc. If the dream is pretty good but contains a few concerning issues, it's probably a heads-up to pay attention to your choices.

## R

Raunchy. These are dreams with some sex, violence, bad language, same-gender kissing, etc. These dreams are usually warning dreams and are meant to get your attention. Sometimes, however, we can simply be processing traumatic issues in life, and they appear as an R-rated dream. Again, our conscience and spirit will know if we are doing something we're not supposed to be doing or if we're simply dealing with some painful and traumatic issues.

## X, XX, XXX

These are sexual dreams. Sex dreams are rarely what you think they are. See the section in Chapter 11, "How to Interpret 21 Symbolic Categories." and look for insights about sex dreams.

## GOD IS IN THE DETAILS!

I've always heard it said, "The devil's in the details." I understand the phrase means we can be easily distracted with minor details that really don't matter, and they may keep us from seeing the most important thing. However, when it comes to studying God's Holy Word and interpreting dreams, I have found that *God* is in the details, and there are amazing hidden rewards to be found if you take the time to meditate on them and why they are included in your dream.

God does nothing without purpose, and let me restate that even though *few* dreams actually come from God, He is the one who created us with the ability to dream. Therefore, it stands to reason that everything in your dream has meaning—no matter the author. Even dreams we get from the enemy of our soul, satan and his demonic realm, have purpose and meaning and reveal things that can be incredibly helpful for us to know.

It is important to focus on the main issues and emotions in your dreams first, but then I implore you to go on a spiritual scavenger hunt to find the buried treasures hidden in the details that are waiting to be found! You'll be amazed and stand in awe of the things God will reveal to you! I've included some of my personal examples in some of the categories listed in Chapter 11, "How to Interpret 21 Symbolic Categories.""

## JEDI DREAM TIPS

- There will always be Scripture for a dream if God is communicating directly with you.

- Titling your dreams specifically, as though they were a book or a movie, will help you interpret most of your dreams.

- Investigate your dreams with lots of questions.

- One word will unlock the entire dream.

- Try several different approaches to interpreting your dreams to see what works best for you.

## JOURNALING YOUR DREAMSCAPES

Journaling your dreams is vital to understanding them. When you're faithful to value what God has given you, you will be given more and clarity will increase. This is a spiritual principle. The ancient Hebraic scrolls reveal this spiritual principle in several places (see Matthew 13:12; Mark 4:25; Luke 8:18; 19:26). The spiritual principle basically is that if God can trust you with little, He will give you more. He will give it to someone who will cherish it and respond to Him.

Something supernatural happens when we take even an abstract thought and commit it to paper. It's as though that action pulls the thought from the invisible realm into the visible one, and it becomes physical matter that can now be acted upon. We see that power over and over for those who write down their goals. Studies have shown the significance of simply writing it down. You may refer to a Harvard Business School study of those who wrote down their goals and those who didn't. There was a study conducted on students in the 1979 Harvard MBA program. In that year, the students were asked if they had set clear, *written goals* for their future and made plans to accomplish them. Only three percent had written goals and plans. Thirteen percent had goals, but not in writing, and 84 percent had no goals at all. Please remember the emphasis on those who *wrote it down*—only three percent. Ten years later they were interviewed again. The findings are amazing. The thirteen percent who had goals were, on average, earning twice as much as the eighty-four percent who had no goals at all. What's more astounding is that the three percent who *wrote down* their goals were earning, on average, ten times as much as the other ninety-seven percent *combined!*

God commanded His people to keep records of many things. When He reveals something, it is to be valued and treated with honor. Look in Habakkuk 2:2-3:

> Then the Lord answered me and said: **"Write the vision and make it plain on tablets**, that he may run who reads it. For the vision is yet for an appointed time; but at the end it will speak, and it will not lie. Though it tarries, wait for it; because it will surely come, it will not tarry."

Ancient writings reveal that Daniel wrote down his dreams, too. Look in Daniel 7:1:

> In the first year of Belshazzar king of Babylon, Daniel had a dream and visions of his head while on his bed. **Then he wrote down the dream, telling the main facts.**

## EXPLORE THE LANDSCAPE OF YOUR DREAMS!

### *Practical Tips for Journaling Your Dreamscapes*

It's imperative to write your dreams down as soon as possible after you wake up so the dream doesn't "fly away" like Scripture indicates. Let's take a look at some simple ways to document the most important parts of your dream.

### Date your dreams!

Make sure to date your dreams for future reference. It will be important to know what else was going on in your life at the time, and you may begin to see patterns to your dreams regarding how long it takes a prophetic dream to come to pass. Whether you decide to use the date of the evening you go to sleep or the date of the next morning, just make sure to keep it consistent. I use the date of the next morning because I find most of my dreams happen after midnight.

### P.I.N. it down!

What's the mood of your dream? Positive, indifferent (neutral), or negative?

It will be important to know if the dream felt positive, indifferent, or negative when interpreting it. The reason it's important to note this immediately after it happens is because if you look back on it weeks and months and even years later, you won't remember how it felt at the time you had it and if you should interpret it as positive, indifferent (neutral), or negative.

**Give your dreams three titles as though they were books, movies, or songs.**

The titles you give your dream will usually summarize the meaning for you. Try to come up with titles immediately upon awakening because the dream will feel fresh and sometimes your spirit will know exactly what it's about. Remember to try and be as specific as possible. If the dream is long, with many scenes, title each scene. Many times the scenes are simply the same message in a different way, or each scene may reveal different issues to pay attention to. Refer back to our section about titling your dreams if you need a refresher.

**Capture the details.**

If you don't have the time to write the entire dream out upon waking, then simply make a bulleted list of ideas, thoughts, symbols, etc., that will jog your memory later. When writing out the complete dream, try to include as many details, thoughts, observations, feelings, etc. as possible. The details will reveal hidden messages!

**Write down in bullet points the events of the day and any main issues you're going through or praying about.**

Your dreams are often about the events of the day or issues you're going through or struggling with. That's why it's important to journal what's going on in real life. You may also want to journal things you've been talking to God about, because many dreams are a direct response to prayers. If you skip this step, you'll find that when you go back and review the dreams later, you may not have a clue as to what they're about because you won't remember what was going on in your life at the time. Dreams are mostly symbolic and, therefore, won't always reveal the specifics of what they pertain to.

**Watch for patterns.**

There are many consistencies and patterns to a dream life. Here are a handful of things to be mindful of:

- When dreams come to pass, pay attention to specifically how long it took after you had the dream. You may discover there is a typical pattern for you personally. Other things you can look for are symbols in the dream that may have revealed how long it would take to come to pass. For example, in two dreams in Scripture, three baskets and three branches meant three days (see Genesis 40).

- Watch for symbols that frequently appear in your dreams. Get our *Dreamscapes® Dream Dictionary* app for phones and tablets to help you interpret your dream symbols. You can request a symbol interpretation if it's not in the dictionary.

- Pay attention to repeated words, people who consistently appear in your dreams, etc.

- Watch the patterns and themes to the titles of your dreams. You may see you have numerous dreams that feel differently, but ultimately have the same theme or issue.

- Pay attention to when you dream; it may align with particular dates. Jesus is a Hebrew and Israel is God's chosen place, so it's not unusual to discover things line up with the Hebraic calendar, important days of the week or month, specific dates, etc.

## JEDI DREAM TIPS

- Expect God to speak to you in dreams.

- Value your dreams!

- Prepare your mind to receive; prepare your bedside with what you need to write.

- Pray and ask God to help you remember.

- Pause before you fully wake up, then write down your dream or bullet points.

- Exhaustion, sleep medications, and illegal drugs can interfere with recalling your dreams.

- If you awake during the night, try to ease back into the dream.

## WHAT NEXT?

Here is a simple ten-step summary to help you process your dreams:

1. Thank God for giving you dreams and helping you remember them. Pray and ask the Holy Spirit to help you understand them.

2. Journal them! (Reread the section titled, "Journaling Your Dreamscapes.")

3. Observe the titles and see if they make sense and match anything else going on in your life right now. Interpret any symbolism in the titles. Keep retitling until they make sense!

4. Do the emotions in the dream match anything you're feeling in real life right now? If so, it's probably an emotional processing dream.

5. Do the actions fit anything going on in your life right now? If so, that's probably what the dream is about.

6. Always ask yourself, *What if every person in my dream was me?* Are there actions or attitudes that need to be addressed? Most dreams are parables (stories that are examples about a truth) and are about the dreamer, and many times the people in the dream—even all of them at the same time—may be showing you aspects about yourself. My rule of thumb is—it never hurts to check yourself first! I've been shocked at how many dreams I thought were about someone else ended up being about *me!*

7. Research symbols, wordplays, the numbers, the people, and the details. I use the following resources:

   - The Bible! I primarily use three sites and they all have free phone apps as well.

- Blueletterbible.org has extensive research tools that are at your fingertips.

- Biblegateway.com—easy to copy and paste.

- Biblestudytools.com—easy to navigate.

- Dictionary.reference.com—An online dictionary.

- Wikipedia.org (not always reliable or credible).

- *The Baby Name Book* by Dorothy Astoria for definitions of names of people who don't have specific symbolism.

- *Dreamscapes® Dream Dictionary* app for symbol interpretations, especially for numbers, colors, etc. The app is available for phones and tablets for both Apple and Android devices. Get links to the specific app at www.gatewaytodreams.com.

- Search engines like Google and Bing.

8. Consider what your response to the dream will be, especially if it was communication from God. For instance, consider if you need to pray, obey, change your attitude, share something with someone, etc.

9. Continue to meditate on it and keep turning the puzzle pieces until they fit!

10. Locate Scripture with the sites mentioned above if the dream feels like it's from God. If God is communicating directly with you, there will always be Scripture associated with the dream!

*Chapter 10*

# THE SECRET GATEWAY: INVITE THE LIGHT

## DREAM ON! ACCELERATE YOUR ABILITY AND DESTINY!

You have now been equipped with the tools you need to excavate the treasures hidden in your dreams. You may ask, "Is there anything else I can do to accelerate my ability to interpret dreams other than studying?" There are some dreams that only a Christian will be able to interpret.

> *"What no eye has seen, what no ear has heard, and what no human mind has conceived"—the things God has prepared for those who love him—these are the things God has revealed to us by his Spirit. The Spirit searches all things, even the deep things of God. For who knows a person's thoughts except their own spirit within them? In the same way no one knows the thoughts of God except the Spirit of God. What we have received is not the spirit of the world, but the Spirit who is from God, so that we may understand what God has freely given us* (1 Corinthians 2:9-12 NIV).

What this says is that only those who have the spirit of God can know the mind of God and be given true understanding. This happens when you are born again, or *from above*, which means your spirit is born anew with the new spirit from God. God reveals secrets to His servants:

> *Let a man so consider us, as servants of Christ and stewards of the mysteries of God* (1 Corinthians 4:1).

> *But His secret counsel is with the upright* (Proverbs 3:32).

> *And they said to him, "We each have had a dream, and there is no interpreter of it." So Joseph said to them, "Do not interpretations belong to God? Tell them to me, please"* (Genesis 40:8).

There is a secret gateway to accelerate your ability to interpret dreams. Jesus Christ is the secret! He is the only Gateway to correct dream interpretation. By having a personal relationship with Jesus and making Him the Lord and Savior of your life, you are plugging yourself into the main power source, and you'll begin to get divine downloads and understanding personally from God! You may wonder, "How do I do that?" The answer is simple—just ask!

## THE BORN (FROM ABOVE) IDENTITY!

> *God is light and in Him is no darkness at all* (1 John 1:5).

This invitation is to all who desire an intimate relationship with God and are compelled to step into the realm of eternity with Him. Receiving His Holy Spirit empowers you and propels you into the realm of the supernatural and a deeper experience of His love.

If you desire His light, His Love, His Holy Spirit, simply humble your heart and with sincerity pray this prayer or a similar plea to God:

*God, I want to live in the eternal and supernatural realm with You. I realize I am a sinner and I cannot come to You and be filled with Your light and Your Holy Spirit unless I believe and acknowledge that Jesus Christ is Your Son and He died on the cross for my sins. I realize He rose from the dead and is with You now in the heavenly realm.*

*Please forgive me of all of my sins (confess as many as you can think of), and I ask You now to fill me with Your Light, Your Love, and Your Holy Spirit. I ask You to fill me with all of You and give me understanding of the destiny You have designed specifically for my life. I will be a true follower and disciple of Jesus Christ and will learn to live, act, and think the way You want me to.*

## CONGRATULATIONS!

You've just been spiritually born from *above!* Now it's time to go *beyond* all you can ask or imagine! The ancient book of Romans confirms that you are born from above if you believe and confess Jesus as your Lord and Savior:

*Because if you acknowledge and confess with your lips that Jesus is Lord and in your heart believe (adhere to, trust in, and rely on the truth) that God raised Him from the dead, you will be saved. For with the heart a person believes (adheres to, trusts in, and relies on Christ) and so is justified (declared righteous, acceptable to God), and with the mouth he confesses (declares openly and speaks out freely his faith) and confirms [his] salvation (Romans 10:9-10 AMP).*

If you have just taken this step of inviting the Spirit of God, His Son, Jesus Christ, into your heart and inviting His Holy Spirit to fill your spirit, would you please let me know? I would love to pray for you and encourage you. Email me at invitethelight@ gatewaytodreams.com.

If you have any questions or don't understand this concept and need further information, please contact my ministry, Above & Beyond, and we will get in touch with you and answer any questions you may have. There is a question/comment submission form on the "request" page of our website at www.gatewaytodreams.com. Also please take time to sign up for our email list and look for other helpful tools and encouraging support on the website.

Remember, *Jesus Christ is the Gateway to your dreams.* He is the Door, the Gate, the Path, the Light, and the *only* way to your spiritual destiny and all that God has for you!

## THE FIELD OF DREAMS: BELIEVE, BEGIN, BECOME!

### *If you build it, they will come—a true lesson in faith!*

Remember the classic movie, *Field of Dreams?* If not, I strongly encourage you to watch it. In 1989, I began working for Universal Pictures, the home video division. A year later, we released *Field of Dreams* on home video (VHS tapes at the time). In brief, it's a story about faith and destiny. It's about a man who hears a voice that says, "If you build it, they will come."

The voice continues to give him simple instructions and it ultimately culminates into him building a supernatural baseball field that thousands come to pay to see from all across the country and the money saves their farm. Much more happens along the way, but the simple message I desire to leave with you is that dream interpretation is similar and requires faith and obedience.

### *Believe!*

First, you have to believe God created you with the ability to dream and that dreams have meaning.

Second, you have to be faithful to write your dreams down and then begin your dream journey to discovery. It will not always be easy. In fact, it may become very frustrating at times. The key is to always remember that *God is the key to understanding everything.* Only God can lead you to a correct interpretation and also give you the wisdom to know how and when to respond.

Last, if you act in faith and remain faithful to value what God gives you, He will give you more! It's a spiritual principle that if you are faithful with little, you'll receive more (see Matthew 25:14-23).

## Begin!

Just start! Place your pad of paper or electronic device beside your bed and write down whatever you remember! Also begin to pay attention to the happenings in your everyday life and begin interpreting them as though they were a dream. You'll discover the Creator of the universe is madly in love with you and is communicating with you all the time!

## Become!

Now it's time to *become* all God created you to be! Interpreting symbolic speech is not just for dreams. God is speaking to you in everything all the time! He adores you and is waiting to be invited into your life in an entirely new way and at a deeper level than you've ever imagined. In parting, I leave you with some "becoming" thoughts:

- Become aware of the fact that God desires to speak to you all the time.

- Become interested in your dreams.

- Become more knowledgeable about the Word of God by spending time in it *every day!*

- Become sensitive to the voice of God—His Holy Spirit—prompting you, convicting you, encouraging you, and guiding you.

- Become more humble each day. Humility is not thinking less of yourself, it's thinking of yourself less and remembering God is God and you are not.

- Become more teachable every day.

- Become willing to be wrong when it comes to interpreting. Even if your interpretation makes logical sense, it may have a different meaning from what you may be aware of.

- Become all God has created you to become!

The most important "become" of all—if you haven't already done so, *become a Christ believer* and receive eternal life with God!

*Section 4*

# SYMBOLOGY: GOD'S SYMBOLIC LOVE LANGUAGE

# Chapter 11

# HOW TO INTERPRET 21 SYMBOLIC CATEGORIES

God gave me a dream many years ago that I would write a book. I didn't have specific instructions about the book, except I presumed it was about dreams. I spent an enormous amount of time interpreting symbols for people and originally thought this book was supposed to be a dream dictionary. The problem with a book of dream symbols is that it can only contain a restricted number of entries and the possibilities for dream symbol meanings are endless.

It wasn't until 2013, when my ministry, Above & Beyond, released our *Dreamscapes® Dream Dictionary* app for phones and tablets, that I realized this book was not supposed to be a dictionary at all and that our app was the answer for that and it could continually evolve. *What a relief!* For ten years I had been overwhelmed with the idea of compiling literally thousands upon thousands of symbols into a book!

The incredible thing about our Dreamscapes® phone and tablet apps are they are ever evolving, and if a symbol is not in the app you can click on "submit request" and we will interpret the symbol for you and put it in the app! The app is for Apple and Android devices, and you can find it where you buy apps!

## TEACH A MAN TO FISH

As discussed in a previous chapter about dream dictionaries, they should only be used to help you brainstorm, because there are very few absolutes and most of them do not have God's perspective. Another issue is that people can become too dependent on them and forget to think about their own personal experiences and consider numerous other interpretations that are not included.

There is a saying, "Give a man a fish, feed him for a day. Teach a man to fish, feed him for life." Instead of giving you a dream dictionary that is basically "giving you a fish," I felt God wanted me to use this book to "teach you to fish" so you could feed yourself! I heard Bobby Conner, who is a prophet of God, say one time that God told him the highest form of treason is when God gives us something and we use it to draw people to us instead of Him (I think I've paraphrased what he said). We need to teach you to fish for yourself so you don't depend on a dream dictionary, a person, a prophet, a dream interpreter, or a ministry, but instead run into the arms of God and discover the hidden treasures for yourself!

After documenting and interpreting over 30,000 of my own dreams, I have discovered my symbols fall into one of 21 categories, which I have included below. In the 21 following sections, I have simply shared some of the things I've learned about how I approach interpreting each of the categories. My desire is to give you some shortcuts and help you begin to think metaphorically. If you know how to approach interpreting the categories, a dream dictionary (preferably our *Dreamscapes® Dream Dictionary* app!) will simply be a quick point of reference and not where you go to depend on your interpretations. *Let's go fishing!*

## ACTIONS AND SITUATIONS

"Actions and situations" is the most obvious category to interpret. Actions and situations in our dreams are often happening in our actual waking life, too, so this category is very often the anchor in your dream that pins it to reality. If the action or situation hasn't happened already in your waking life, it may be wise to stay alert because it could possibly be something that is to happen in the future. Pay attention to the words you choose to write down. If they are future tense, it may reveal it's yet to come. If it's past or present tense, you're probably just processing the issues.

Begin by looking at the action verbs in the dream that you have written down. Action verbs are words that show action in the past, present, or future tense. Examples: run, running, ran; talk, talking, talked; help, helping, helped; etc., or they can be words such as *went* (somewhere), *left* (to go somewhere), etc. Just remember, verbs show the action in the dream.

Situations can also be categorized as issues or problems. Look for these in each dream. These can often be the titles of the dream that summarize what the entire dream is about. For instance, example situations or issues could be problems with the neighbor, going to the bathroom in public, my car is not working, etc. They don't always have to be a problem, though! Sometimes they are things such as an encounter with a dolphin or a visitation from God or I got a brand-new car.

There are also thousands of actions and situations that are actually figures of speech. We already discussed figures of speech; now let's take a look at some examples of both actions and situations to help you spot them:

- Sitting on a fence may be an idiom (saying) meaning to be indecisive, such as, "I'm sitting on the fence about whether to go on the trip or not."

- Backing out of a driveway may reveal backing out of a commitment.

- Running away from something or someone may reveal avoiding issues; or in the positive, it may reveal running from temptations.

- Stuck somewhere may indicate a feeling of being stuck in a situation, choice, relationship, etc.

- Jumping off a diving board may mean taking a leap of faith or diving right into something, such as work, a relationship, a responsibility, etc.

## ANIMALS

Animals in a dream usually represent behavior—either that of the dreamer or that of people in your life you're observing or dealing with. Take a look at the specific animal and see what it is doing and how it is acting, and then ask yourself if you or anyone you know is acting this way.

Animals can also have hidden insights. For instance, a porcupine. I once spoke to a middle school class about dream interpretation on career day. One little boy had a porcupine in his dream. I had no idea what a porcupine meant, and instantly the Holy Spirit told me it often means writing, because the quills can represent a quill pen that you write with. So instead of approaching it as a matter of fact, I simply asked the boy, "Do you like to write?"

He said, "Oh my goodness! How did you know that!" I told him I felt God told me, and that I believed he had a gift from God. You would not believe how excited this boy was! Remember, context is the key. In the right contexts, a porcupine can also mean someone who is defensive in nature and can be sharp with their words, or it may even represent something like quilting or needlework because of their needles, etc.

The first thing I do with an animal is look it up in Scripture to see if it's there and how God used the animal in different contexts. For instance, a lion can represent Jesus in Revelation 5:5. However, satan is also *compared* to a lion in the Bible in First Peter 5:8 (notice, he's not actually mentioned as the lion itself!). Always check the Bible first. Then the next thing I do is look it up in the encyclopedia to see what its behavior patterns are and other miscellaneous things it says about the animal, insect, or creature. You will be amazed at what you discover that makes the dream make so much sense! Online encyclopedias make research quick and easy. It's especially important to do further research on an animal if it was a specific type, from a specific region of the world, etc. For example, if instead of just writing *dog* you write *golden retriever* or *poodle*, it's important to know why it was so specific.

I have often found that most insects represent the demonic realm, though not always! Sometimes they can represent things like wisdom, as stated in Proverbs about the ant. If you really want understanding, don't just look at the *what* (in this case that the ant can represent wisdom), but also meditate on the *why* (because they are diligent, they do things without being told, and they plan for the future). On the other hand, if you're at a picnic, ants *are* demonic—LOL! Ants can represent a ton of little things that are irritating and things that really get on your nerves. Look at the size, description, and attributes of the animal, insect, or creature and that will help you determine which direction to go.

## BEVERAGES, FOOD, PHARMACY

### Beverages

This can be a very difficult dream category to interpret. Let's take a look at the basic verbs first, such as drink (as you would a beverage). Metaphorically speaking, to swallow something or to drink something means to take it in or believe it. Sometimes it's not *that* you're drinking but it's *what* you're drinking, how you respond to it in the dream, if it's good or bad, etc. Again and again, *context is always the key to a correct interpretation.* What you are drinking will sometimes simply give you more clarity on the issue.

Remember, *always consult Scripture first!* For instance, there are beverages in the Bible, such as wine or milk. Metaphors are used extensively in Scripture, so don't neglect looking there first. For example, milk can mean things that are easy to understand, believe, and/or swallow. We give a baby milk to drink because it is easily digested. This metaphor for milk is often used in Scripture concerning new or immature believers. Meat, on the other hand, represents things that are tougher or more difficult to understand or consume. Why? Because it takes longer to eat it because you have to chew on it, you have to be mature and have teeth, etc. To chew on something is a saying that means to meditate on something for a while.

## Food

There are lots of types of food in Scripture—and in dreams. Sometimes in Scripture food will be a metaphor for much more abstract things. For example, many times fruit is used symbolically for character attributes, such as the fruit of the Spirit—peace, love, joy, patience (longsuffering), kindness, goodness, faithfulness, gentleness, and self-control as listed in Galatians 5:22-23. The fruit of the Spirit is also mentioned as being in all goodness, righteousness, and truth in Ephesians 5:9, and Scripture speaks of people "producing" whatever is in their heart. The Bible goes on to explain one kind of tree cannot produce another tree's fruit—that the tree will only produce the type of fruit that comes from the type of tree it is. If you do a more in-depth study of what word is used for fruit in Scripture, you will discover that the definitions provide intriguing and more specific insight. Definitions for *fruit* in the Bible:

A. The fruit of the trees, vines, of the fields

B. The fruit of one's loins, his progeny, his posterity

That which originates or comes from something, an effect, result:

A. Work, act, deed

B. Advantage, profit, utility

C. Praises, which are presented to God as a thank offering

D. To gather fruit (example: a reaped harvest) into life eternal (as into a granary), is used in figurative discourse to those who by their labours have fitted souls to obtain eternal life.[1]

There are millions of different beverages and foods, so just as any other symbol, first look at the attributes of the item and also ask what it might remind you of personally, because sometimes we have experiences with things or memories of them that come into play when interpreting dreams. For instance, it may be a food you love or hate, and that might affect your interpretation because we each have our own dream language. Also consider the condition and/or the color, size, and if it tastes good or bad, is ripe, etc.

## Pharmacy

In dream interpretation, pharmacy is handled slightly different from beverages or food. Once again, consider what else is going on in the dream. Also consider if it is a legal or illegal drug. Illegal drugs usually represent rebellion, as well as the abuse of prescription drugs. With that said, it's more important to look at the function of the drug. Also pay attention to see if it is a prescription or an over-the-counter type of drug. This will tell you the seriousness of it. For instance, if it is pink Pepto Bismol, it may represent that all you need is a little love to make you feel better. Why? Because Pepto Bismol makes the stomach feel better if it's upset. Pink can often represent love, and the stomach usually represents the heart. It may be this scenario simply represents being "upset," and a little love will make you feel better. However, if it's a prescription drug, it will clearly give you an indication to pay more serious attention. When interpreting prescription drugs, though they are usually symbolic, we also have to take into consideration that it may be a literal anchor revealing something in real life or an issue surrounding something that we are taking. One other thing to note is to pay attention to the names of things, because you may often find wordplays. Food and pharmacy also include herbs, etc.

## BODY PARTS, BODILY FUNCTIONS, HEALTH ISSUES

This category contains body parts, such as arms, legs, eyes, etc. It also contains bodily functions and health issues, such as baldness, arthritis, pregnancy, vomiting, etc. Ancient Scripture is filled with meanings in this category. There are even divine mysteries explaining how those who believe in Jesus as the Christ, the only Son of God, are considered "parts" of His body. We are the arms, legs, eyes, etc., and we all have a different function. God's attributes are also seen in body parts, such as His arm, His breath, etc. Let's take a quick look at how to approach this category with the understanding to always check Scripture first.

### Body Parts

When you discover that a body part is mentioned in Scripture, it's important to see not only what it means, but *why*. This will give you a deeper revelation of why it may be in a dream, and it will give your heart understanding of God's ways.

Consider the purpose and function of the specific body part. For instance, an eye sees. Metaphorically, this may have to do with how you the dreamer is "seeing" or perceiving something. It may be your outlook on an issue or situation—your perspective. The eye can also represent being prophetic, which means getting specific information from God and telling others. The prophetic usually helps with what will happen in the future, so the eye symbolically represents "seeing" into the future or "seeing" what God is showing you.

Consider the condition of the body part and if it's functioning properly. This will give you clues not only to the issue, but perhaps also the answer to a problem. For example, if the eye is having problems seeing, maybe it reveals you need to adjust your perspective. The answer in real life would be to correct the vision somehow—either with glasses, contacts, or Lasik surgery (unless something else specific was mentioned in the dream). Symbolically, correcting your vision may mean to choose to see something in a better way, with a better attitude. If you have to get glasses in the dream, are they nearsighted or farsighted? Nearsighted may reveal the need to focus on the here and now and not worry about the future, for instance. Farsighted, on the other hand, may indicate you are a visionary and can see far-off, or it may reveal the need to focus on the future going forward, and stop worrying about the past or present.

### Bodily Functions

Many times the bodily functions, such as vomiting, going to the bathroom, etc., also fall under the category of actions and situations. Think through the function and why it's happening. As I've mentioned many times before, the *why* may be more important than the *what*.

If someone is vomiting in a dream, for instance, do you know why? Did the person eat something bad? Is the person crying or drinking alcohol? The *why* will give you a more specific interpretation. For example, if it was bad food, you could interpret the food first. Food in general may be things that you've eaten or consumed symbolically, such as teachings that "didn't agree with you" or that you didn't agree with. It may also be that someone told you something (the food) and it caused you to reject it. Our bodies vomit as a result of the body knowing how to heal itself sometimes, so perhaps you needed to respond in a specific way to get rid of toxic things.

I have also found that vomiting often has to do with rejection issues—feeling rejected or actually being rejected. Let's take a look at vomiting because of alcohol as another example. Alcohol in dreams also means being wrongly influenced by others. Again, this is most likely a rejection issue and feeling rejected by others.

If the vomit is being thrown up on someone else, it may reveal that you're vomiting up too much information (gossip, etc.), or it can also represent bringing up old issues having to do with someone else—"throwing up" the past or throwing up old issues over and over, for instance. Vomiting can also represent reacting in anger or other strong emotions instead of reacting how God says to react. In medicine, to react to a medicine is bad and to respond to treatment is good. I have found it to be the same in dreams under the correct context.

## Health Issues

Health issues can be things like cancer, kidney stones, a broken bone, etc. Did you know that cancer is actually in the Bible? It always amazes me at the things I find are actually in there that I never realized before. Cancer in Scripture represents things like idle words, ungodliness, lies, gossip, slander, unforgiveness, bitter words, etc.—ungodly things that only bring harm to yourself and eat away at you (see 2 Timpthy 2:17).

Cancer can also represent a demonic attack against the body of Christ or against the dreamer. I recently had a dream where I had cancer and God revealed it was a ton of things that were an attack against me from someone I loved dearly. In the dream I had to endure chemo in order to be healed. Chemo represented having to take "harsh treatment." I wasn't sure in the dream how my body was going to respond to the treatment and if I would throw up or not. That was an indication letting me know I was about to be harshly treated by someone I loved and that I had a choice if I was going to respond or react to the person's treatment of me. I could react in anger and bitterness, or I could respond in a godly way. In the dream I was healed quickly, and I responded correctly! In real life I did, too!

## BRANDS, COMPANIES, ORGANIZATIONS

This is a super fun category! It took me a while, but I eventually figured out that for companies or brands, it's often their slogan that is the hidden insight to find and pay attention to!

The first time I discovered this was with the dreams I had about my Honda Accord—"all in one accord" (unity, see Acts 1:14)—and their slogan is "The power of dreams"! Isn't that amazing? The car represented unity, but it also represented me doing dream interpretation and the power of that! I think it's also amazing it was not just a dream, but that I was literally driving something that represented my dreams and unity—and it wasn't only in a dream. What do you think the chances of that are without me knowing in advance what their slogan was?

I've also had dreams about Disney, and their slogan is, "Where dreams come true." Something else amazing happened to me regarding this in real life. My ministry name is Above & Beyond. About a year prior to my founding of Above & Beyond, I bought a Lexus 300 instead of the Honda Accord. One of the main focuses I have at Above & Beyond is to present God in an excellent light and to convey to others that He goes above and beyond all people can ask or even imagine, according to Ephesians 3:20. While driving down the highway one day after I had begun my ministry, Above & Beyond, I glanced to my right and saw a huge Lexus billboard, and it said, "Above and Beyond: The Passionate Pursuit of Excellence." I had no idea that my car slogan was above and beyond before that dream, and it was after I had started my ministry. Coincidence? I think not! God is amazing, and you will find as you interpret your dreams that you can apply the same principles to interpret the voice of God throughout your life! You can say to your life, "If this were a dream, what would it mean?"

## BUILDINGS, BUILDING ELEMENTS, ROOMS, FURNITURE

### Buildings

Buildings are things like houses, stores, offices, warehouses, etc. Here are some quick guidelines when interpreting buildings:

1. Consider the purpose or function of the building. This will tell you what it's probably about. For instance, is it the home you grew up in as a child? Consider your memories and thoughts about the place and what else it might represent to you personally. If it's a warehouse, what size is the warehouse and what does it store?

2. Consider the size. The size often speaks to the size of the issue or situation.

3. Does this building exist in real life or just the dream? If it exists in real life, it may be that it has to do with what it represents to you personally. If it doesn't exist in real life, it probably is conveying the idea of the purpose of the building. For example, if it's an office-supply retail store, perhaps it has to do with work or getting supplies you need to get to work or to do work or something more metaphorical like "working" through an issue or situation.

4. Pay attention to the details such as if the building is the same in real life as it is in the dream or if there are things that are entirely different.

## Building Elements

Building elements are things that belong to or are necessary in creating a building—foundation, walls, columns, crown molding, light fixtures, etc. When interpreting these elements, always consider their purpose. The description of them is important as well. For instance, if it's the foundation, is it in good shape or is it cracked? A foundation could be things like trust, or, if in ministry, it could be things like your theology about Jesus Christ, because God wants to build on the foundation of Jesus Christ as Lord and Savior. The condition of it will give you insight if it's positive or negative. I often have very detailed crown molding in my dreams. The crown molding to me represents the enormous number of details I interpret for dream interpretation. The reason is because crown molding is not necessary, but it is incredibly beautiful and really adds value to the entire room. The more detail the crown molding has, the more it reveals how much God is pleased with the interpretation I give of the details in dreams. He also revealed that because teeth can represent relationships or understanding in general, "dental" crown molding often represents that, too— *understanding* the details of dream interpretation or the details of a relationship.

## Rooms

Rooms are typically their function on a symbolic level. For instance, because the kitchen is a place of preparation, it usually represents that something is about to happen that you need to get prepared for. The kitchen is also the heart of the home, and in the correct context it can represent your heart about a matter in your life. Living rooms usually have to do with what's currently going on in your life—what you are currently "living." In real life, bathrooms are where we go to take care of personal things like going to the bathroom, taking a shower, brushing our hair and teeth, etc. In dreams, bathrooms usually represent processing things privately or inwardly, such as emotions, thoughts, etc.

## Furniture

I know I am being redundant, but once again, when inter-preting furniture, just as in other symbols, consider its primary function first. Also take into consideration the details about it, the condition of it, if it's being used or neglected, if it's in the appropriate place, etc. It can get tricky because in Scripture I believe furniture can be representative of wisdom and knowledge according to Proverbs 24:3-4, "Through wisdom a house is built, and by understanding it is established; by knowledge the rooms are filled with all precious and pleasant riches."

Other things to consider are things like the shape of the furniture, the type of material it's made out of, etc. For instance, a square can represent justice because in a square all sides are equal, or it may represent things to do within the world because a square has four corners and the world is referred to as having four corners. However, if you have a rectangular coffee table instead of a square one, rectangles often have to do with money, though not always. God revealed that to me in a dream once that conference tables often represented money because conference tables were often in businesses, which would represent making money. God gave me the Scripture about how Jesus turned over the tables of the mon-eychangers (see Matthew 21:12).

Another interesting example is refrigerators. It took me a while to figure out vacuum cleaners and refrigerators until I noticed the description of them. There are two types of refrigerators. One is upright and horizontally split, and the other is a side-by-side and is vertically split. There are numerous interpretations for each type of refrigerator and other things need to be considered also such as the color, etc.

I eventually discovered that whenever I use the word "upright," whether it be with vacuum cleaners or refrigerators, it represented someone's heart that was upright, which means of good intention or motive. That doesn't mean a side-by-side refrigerator isn't a positive interpretation also. Side by side can represent equally divided, divided on an issue, or it can mean unity or coming "alongside" someone. Also the fact that it is split vertically can be a positive thing as well. Most of the time when I see things that are vertical, it represents from Heaven to earth or coming from God. Whenever I see things that are horizontal, it often represents things that are on earth, which is not necessarily bad. Can you see how the details really do matter?

You could go on to interpret the color of the refrigerator, keeping in mind that if it is the color of your actual refrigerator it may not play into the interpretation. For instance, my refrigerator is black, but that doesn't mean it's bad. It just means my actual refrigerator in real life is black. Black can also mean strong, hidden, and many other things. Because I have a heart for Africa, a black refrigerator can represent my heart for Africa or African/black people. Do you see how important it is to have the full and complete context of not only what is in the dream but what is your opinion and how important it is to include your real-life filters? There's no way you could know I have a heart for Africa unless I tell you. If I don't tell you, there's no way you can interpret the dream to mean that, unless the rest of the dream specifically reveals it. This is why it's imperative to ask tons of questions.

## CLOTHING, ACCESSORIES, JEWELRY

### Clothing

Most of the time clothing represents attitudes, mantles, or character traits. The Bible says to "clothe" yourself with righteousness, with humility, with the fruits of the Spirit, etc. There are mentions also of people who are clothed in shame, etc. When interpreting clothing, take into consideration what piece of clothing it is, the color, size, or if it has a pattern or nationality to it. Often clothes that represent specific countries or nationalities may reveal you have been given the ability to influence that part of the world or people of that nationality. As I stated before, whenever I see something and it's specifically vertical, like vertical stripes on a piece of clothing, it usually represents from Heaven to earth—from God. Horizontal stripes, on the other hand, may reveal having influence in the earth or the world, or in a negative context would represent being of the world or having worldly thoughts, attitudes, or actions, etc. Clothing with patterns usually reveal a *pattern* of thought or action. Mantles are specific abilities and responsibilities God gives a person.

## Accessories

Accessories can be things like belts, ties, hats, shoes, etc. Many of these examples are listed in Scripture, believe it or not! As always, consider what part of the body the accessory is for, if there is Scripture for it, the condition or description of the details, etc. Shoes may have to do with what you're "walking out" in your life or what your career is, etc. Scripture refers to a belt as truth, "Stand firm then, with the belt of truth" (Ephesians 6:14 NIV). Belts can also represent feeling "strapped" financially or using words to beat up somebody (belting them) with the truth. Look for tons of wordplays, riddles, and interesting insights when interpreting this category.

## Jewelry

Jewelry is mentioned throughout Scripture. It speaks of earrings, gemstones, rings, bracelets, etc. As always, seeing jewelry in your dream depends on context to reveal if its appearance is positive or negative. For instance, jewelry can mean obedience if worn on the ears because ears hear, which can mean obey. Jewelry can also mean vain or outward beauty instead of integrity and inward beauty. Remember to always consider the function of the jewelry, where it is worn, why it's being worn, the color, shape, type of gemstone, type of metal, condition of it, etc.

## COLORS AND LIGHT

### Colors

This dream category is self-explanatory. The key is finding godly, biblical examples because there are a lot of sources that falsely interpret colors, which will lead you to a wrong interpretation—one that is not godly. The Bible mentions many colors. I recommend you get our phone or tablet app to save time in finding godly interpretations for colors. You can find links to the app at www.gatewaytodreams.com.

In order to find deeper meaning to colors, you can also look into the details such as the hues, tones, if it's dingy or bright, pastel or neon, etc. *Everything* has meaning! Neon, for instance, can represent the soulish or the demonic realm versus the spirit realm because neon comes from black light instead of white. In the right context, however, neon can represent literal things. Because a neon sign tries to get your attention, the neon item in the dream may simply be trying to get your attention to caution you about something. The specific color and what the sign says will give you additional insight.

### Light

What do I mean by light? I mean the amount of light in a dream and the type of light. There are numerous types of light, such as natural sunlight, black lights, CFL, LED, incandescent, fluorescent, high-intensity discharge (HID), etc.

Then there are different types of bulbs under each category, such as halogen. Consider also the details such as the shape of bulb, if it's clear or frosted, and what type of fixture—lamp, ceiling fan, chandelier, curio cabinet, etc. The more details you have, the easier it is to correctly interpret.

Some have said that dreams that are not light and bright are not from God. I completely disagree with that teaching as I've previously mentioned. I've discovered that sometimes when a dream is lacking light, it simply means there needs to be more understanding or truth because light most often represents the truth. A dark dream may simply reveal that the dreamer may be going through a dark time and is in need of understanding. Context, context, context.

## CONDITION, DESCRIPTION, EMOTIONS

All three of these areas—condition, description, emotions—usually represent your emotions. Because most dreams are processing our emotions, these are critical words to look for when you write about your dream. I would say 80 to 90 percent of your dreams are about your emotions and processing them. Therefore, when you interpret your dreams, one thing you can do is highlight all the words that are describing the condition of something, the description of something, or obvious emotions like fear or joy. If these do not line up with what is going on currently in your life or what you've been processing from the past, then it may be about something on the horizon or it may have to do with someone else, so stay alert.

### Condition and Description

The condition and description of something are the descriptive words or adjectives used to describe the dream or the elements in the dream, such as *rusty, bent out of shape, dingy, neglected, abandoned, deflated, inflated*, etc. Can you see how you can feel like these things? Ever felt "rusty" at doing something because you hadn't done it in a while, like riding a bike? Rusty could also indicate something has been neglected or not taken care of. This may reveal a relationship, a person who has been neglected, an area of responsibility, etc. Dingy may reveal that something needs clarity. Neglected or abandoned may be literal, such as being abandoned by a parent or spouse, or feeling neglected by them, etc. Inflated and deflated may reveal how you're feeling, such as an inflated ego or feeling encouraged, while deflated may reveal exhaustion or "tired," feeling like someone let you down, or "took all the air out" of your expectations.

### Emotions

Emotions within a dream are obvious—they are the feelings happening inside the dream such as joy, love, fear, frustration, worry, excitement, peacefulness, etc. The first thing I do with emotions in the dream is ask myself if I currently feel this way anywhere in my life right now. The answer is usually yes. If so, this usually reveals the dream is a processing one.

## DATE, MEASUREMENT, TIME

### Date

Dates include things like specific dates, months, days, holidays, etc. I have found that when specific months are mentioned in a dream, it usually represents either a literal anchor in time for you, or it represents the holiday that happens in that month. For instance, if something is happening in a specific month you're aware of—like a family reunion, starting a new job, etc.—then it may be a reference to that or about what I call the "anchor" to reality. When interpreting holidays, make sure to consider what country you're in because all countries do not celebrate the same holidays.

Here are some quick things I've discovered about some obvious months from an American viewpoint:

- February usually represents love because of Valentine's Day.

- March may be a wordplay for "go ahead and march forward" on a decision, especially if it's March 4 (March forth). March is also when spring begins and can, therefore, represent something new blooming, such as a business, relationship, etc.

- April sometimes represents owing something to God or people because of the April 15 deadline to file taxes. Sometimes it represents vows made, tithes and offerings that are owed to God, etc.

- May usually represents something to do with a mom or the church because of Mother's Day. It's also Memorial Day, so it "may" have to do with remembering and honoring someone.

- June usually represents something to do with fathers because of Father's Day. It may also be about graduating to another spiritual level because many school graduations happen in June.

- July, for America, usually represents independence because of July 4, Independence Day. Independence may simply mean spiritual freedom, or it may reveal becoming more independent, being too independent, etc., depending on context.

- October usually represents either the harvest of souls, meaning eternal spiritual rebirth as a result of believing in Jesus Christ, or it often represents rebellion and witchcraft because of Halloween.

- November is often representative of being grateful because of Thanksgiving. It also may represent being chosen by God for specific service to Him because Election Day is the first Tuesday of November. Election Day may represent God's "elect" people.

- December frequently represents either believing in Jesus Christ, because we celebrate His birth on December 25, or it may represent our spiritual gifts because we give gifts to each other at Christmas;

God gave us His Son as a gift, but He has also given each of us specific spiritual gifts.

These are not all the months, but hopefully they will give you some insight for how to approach interpreting months and holidays.

### Measurement

Measurements can sometimes represent the length of things, such as time. When you notice this, it can be a very subtle insight and hidden key to your dream. Typically when you write your dreams, you don't initially write these sorts of details. For example, how long something is, how many feet or how many inches it is, how far away something was, if it was long-sleeve or short-sleeve shirt, etc., but the length and distance of things can be hidden keys to interpreting how long something has gone on, or how long it will be until it comes to pass. At times, the numbers you use in the length of things are also metaphorical or symbolic. For instance, if it is 12 inches or 12 feet long, it may be more about the number 12, representing authority.

The size of things, such as rooms, objects, etc., can also be included in the measurement category. When you notice the size of certain things, it often speaks of how large an issue is. For instance, if a rectangular conference table can represent money, then the size of it may indicate how big the issue is. If you know exactly how big or small something is by specific measurement, then you can also interpret the numbers metaphorically.

### Time

Time is very interesting, both in dreams and in real life. Very often when you wake up from a dream, you'll notice a specific time on your clock. This can be incredibly important. When you have what feels like a very important dream, the time on the clock is often very strategic and important, especially if you keep seeing the same time over and over. To see the same time repeatedly is usually a sign that God is trying to get your attention. Time on a clock or numbers in a dream can often represent a chapter and verse in the Bible! It's like a spiritual scavenger hunt to decode hidden messages from God. Don't forget that numbers can be symbolic is well. For instance, 11 o'clock can simply mean the eleventh hour, as in not much time left, or it may represent all the other meanings of the number. The very fact that it is time probably reveals it is a reference to time. Once again, I will encourage you to get our Dreamscapes® phone or tablet app for a quick and easy reference to the meaning of specific numbers.

## DIRECTION AND GEOMETRIC SHAPES

### Direction

Directions are North, South, East, West, up, down, sideways, diagonal, etc. As always, you want the interpretation the Bible gives for North, South, East, and West. Many times "up" means heavenly or having to do with looking at things positively, as in, "Things are looking up." Sometimes down means the opposite.

### Geometric Shapes

Geometric shapes are circles, squares, triangles, hexagons, etc. There are many hidden insights to shapes in dreams. For instance, a circle usually represents fellowship or commitment because it is unending. For a great example of why a circle can mean commitment, take a look at the symbolism of wedding rings. As always, remember to check ancient Scripture first because there are numerous shapes mentioned with specific purposes.

If there is a shape with specific sides in your dream, consider the number of sides and that specific number's meaning. Also take into consideration the name and definition of the shape. Many times the definition will reveal hidden treasures. You may find as you're reading the definition of a specific shape that it will have a dual meaning that relates to something else in life. Also take into consideration if it's being used as a noun, verb, or adjective, because each will have its own meaning. The last thing to remember is to ask yourself—are there any wordplays or figures of speech used with a symbol or, in this case, a shape?

A great example is the *square*. The simple definition of a square as a noun can be a quadrilateral with four equal sides and four right angles. When interpreting a square, it may represent justice because all sides are equal. It may also speak of doing the right thing because all angles are "right"—taking an "angle" (or approach) that is correct or right.

As a verb, square can mean to reduce, as in "square off," or to test with measuring devices for deviation from a right angle, straight line, or plane surface. It can also mean to settle or balance a matter, such as in evening the score, paying a bill, or returning a favor. Metaphorically speaking, to reduce or make even may represent humbling someone or reduce them to size. It may also symbolically reveal someone is being tested to see if they are deviating from what is right or just. To even the score may reveal justice, or it may be a negative interpretation of revenge if the context of the dream points in that direction. It may also indicate an issue in the dreamer's life needs to be settled. Do you see how the definitions can have a literal and metaphorical meaning? These are the hidden treasures you'll unearth as you go on your dream digs.

As an adjective, square means to be equal. As an adverb, it can mean fairly and honestly or directly and straightforwardly. The details of the dream indicate how to interpret a square. You'll begin to discover many meanings can all be correct at the same time!

Square is also used in phrases and idioms:

- To *square away* can mean to prepare, get ready, assume an offensive or defensive position, or to put in order. It can also be a nautical term meaning to arrange the yards so as to sail before the wind.

▪ To *square off* can mean to assume a posture of either offense or defense, as in sports; to prepare to dispute with another, as in a court case; or show signs of opposition or resistance.

▪ To *square up* means to settle or pay an account or bill.

▪ *On the square* is an idiom meaning honest, just, or straightforward.

▪ *Out of square* means in disagreement, incorrect, or irregular.

▪ *Square the circle* means to attempt the impossible or strive without any chance of succeeding.

▪ To *square your shoulders* means to prepare for adversity.

▪ If a person is referred to as *a square*, it indicates someone who is uncool, old-fashioned, conservative, or someone who is uninterested in or ignorant of current fads, etc.

Isn't it amazing how many different possibilities there are for one symbol? Always check the Bible first, then delve into dictionaries, the Internet, etc.

# EVENTS, HOBBIES, SPORTS

## Events

Events are usually special occasions, celebrations, appointments, etc. The key to interpreting dream events is to decide if it's literal or symbolic. Sometimes it can be both at the same time.

The type of event tells you to what it's referring. For instance, if it's a work-related event, it's probably about work. Always keep in mind that dreams are symbolic, so even though something may be about work in the dream, it may also have a duplicate meaning. For example, work may be a parallel to something else in your life that needs *work* and not necessarily about your actual job.

## Sports

When interpreting sports, keep in mind the objective of the sport. You'll also find many hidden wordplays with the terms used in each sport. Let's look at a handful of examples.

### Tennis

I remember the first time I had tennis in a dream. I laughed hysterically as the Lord showed me what it meant. He told me that tennis usually represents loving and serving because tennis begins with a score of "love" and you have to "serve" the ball.

### Soccer

When approaching a sport, begin by brainstorming the terms used in each sport. For instance, soccer has terms about using your head, scoring a goal, being a forward, kicking the ball around, etc. I recently interpreted a dream for someone with soccer in it. The gentleman shared that he was at work and playing soccer with his co-workers. It turned out that soccer represented "kicking around some ideas," "using his head" at work, and being on a "team" with other people to attain a similar "goal."

### Football (American)

Football usually has to do with "tackling" difficult issues or situations. Also look for words like *pass, toss, defensive, offensive, goal,* the *uprights,* etc. The meaning of these can represent life situations such as "passing" on an opportunity, "tossing" around ideas, being "defensive" about something, "offending" someone, initiating or "tackling" something, or achieving a "goal" by being "upright," etc.

### Basketball

Basketball usually has to do with "taking a shot" at getting your "point" across to others. It may also represent being grateful, because God's Word says to enter His "courts" with thanksgiving (see Psalm 100:4). Also pay attention to how many points the shot scored. The number itself has meaning.

## *Hobbies*

Hobbies can include fishing, which is also a sport, quilting, walking, exercising, scrapbooking, etc. Even though some of these things are sports, they are also considered hobbies to those who simply enjoy them and don't compete in them. Hobbies are to be interpreted in a similar way to sports. Look for wordplays and consider the objective of the hobby. If it's exercising, for instance, is there another area of your life that you're *exercising* something, like faith or your authority? Remember to maintain metaphorical or symbolic thinking when interpreting.

## GEOGRAPHICAL LOCATIONS AND PLACEMENT

### *Geographical Locations*

Geographical locations are states, cities, countries, etc. They can also be things like hills, fields, roads, etc. The following are insights I've discovered about this category:

*Countries* in dreams tend to be what they are known for. Here are a few brief examples, remembering there is always a positive and negative possibility for every symbol, and your personal opinion and experiences will also affect your interpretation.

- *United States*: Freedom and courage, because it is considered the land of the free and home of the brave. Until recently, the United States was also known as a Christian nation under God, but sadly we have severely compromised those values. As a result, the US may also represent compromise.

- *China*: Humility and honor, because that is its culture. China may also represent persecution of Christians or control.

- *England*: Usually represents the United Kingdom of God—Christian believers!

- *India*: Usually represents unbelief in God and Jesus because Hindus worship so many gods and they don't believe in the one true God. It often represents idolatry because of that, too.

- *Mexico*: Hard work, because its people are known for intense labor and work ethic. In the negative, I have found Mexico to represent the drug cartel, which could be interpreted as a very high level of spiritual warfare including the demonic and possibly drug abuse.

Keep in mind that your opinion will heavily influence the interpretation and there is a positive and negative option for every symbol, even though I haven't necessarily included both for each country just mentioned. Also keep in mind countries can be literal if you have an assignment there for work or from God.

- *States*: States usually have to do with their state slogan that is on the license plate. I've also found it helpful to look at the names of the state sports teams and other state symbols.

- *Cities*: They usually represent their slogan, their reputation, or major things in the city such as rivers, parks, buildings, and other attractions. There can also be wordplays in this category. For instance, I grew up in St. Charles, Illinois. Whenever St. Charles is in my dreams, it represents Christians because one of its slogans is "The Home of the Saints." Christians are also referred to as "the saints" (see Ephesians 4:12).

## Placement

The key to discovering what I mean by placement is to look for words including *in, on, around, behind, above, below*, etc. There are many wordplays in this category. For instance, "on the fence" and "in the middle of the road" are both figures of speech or idioms meaning undecided or neutral. Take into consideration the object of focus in your dream, such as what you're in, on, or around—like a rock, mountain, road, etc.

## MEDIA AND MUSICAL INSTRUMENTS

Media are books, movies, music, television, games, etc. Let's take a quick look at some aspects to consider when encountering media in your dreams.

### Books

Pay attention to the title. It may be a wordplay or have obvious or hidden meaning. Consider the main characters or the main theme.

### Movies

- Does the title have any obvious or hidden meaning?

- Is the title a wordplay?

- Pay attention to the famous people in the movie. It may have to do with their real or fictional personality.

- What is the movie about?

### Television

*Television* is often a wordplay for *tell-a-vision*. If it is a vision, it means "watch" what's happening on the television because it will come to pass. Consider what program is on the television in the dream. For instance, if it is a game show, series, soap opera, talk show, etc. Each has a specific meaning discussed in our *Dreamscapes® Dream Dictionary* app for phones and tablets. Two examples: a soap opera may indicate some "drama" going on in your life, and a talk show may reveal a topic that needs to be discussed or influencing people with what you say, etc.

### Games—Video and Board Games

- Depends on the type of game. What is it rated? The more negative the rating, the more it may reveal the seriousness of an issue.

- It may represent prayer strategies if it's a video game. Why? Because you use a thumb for video games and the thumb often represents prayer. Playing games successfully also requires strategy.

- It may be a literal element that indicates the game you are playing is negatively impacting your life. Some games actually open the door to a demonic attack, such as Dungeons and Dragons and Pokémon.

- Consider the name of the game and the purpose or goal.

### Music

Music is an interesting category. I find that music is not only relevant in your dreams, but you will often wake up and hear lyrics of a song in your head. These are important to pay attention to because sometimes it's God speaking to you! Many times I've prayed before I've gone to bed, and when I woke up the answer was in the lyrics to a song, or the song that was playing in my head was encouragement or worship to God from my spirit to Him.

I will share a good example that was not a dream, but it could've been and is just as relevant to what I'm talking about. One time while I was teaching at a women's retreat about how God communicates, I mentioned that God can speak through music and songs. I went on to give examples of the titles of songs having specific meaning sometimes, and one woman began to weep and cry and giggle as she discovered that God had been speaking to her!

She shared how she had a very formal music room in her house. It had white carpet, a grand piano, and many other instruments. On the wall behind the couch she had hung a picture of Elvis Presley dressed in his signature white jumpsuit. She shared how everyone thought the picture of Elvis did not fit in that room because it was so formal and the picture of Elvis seemed inappropriate. She was constantly ridiculed but couldn't find it within her to take the picture down and didn't even know why. After I shared how God can speak through music, the picture flashed in her mind and she said she realized why she could never take the picture down. She explained how every time she went into that room and saw the picture of Elvis, she would hear him singing the hymn, "How Great Thou Art." Tears streamed down her face as she realized that she worshiped God every time she stepped into the room as she too would sing "How Great Thou Art." Elvis is also considered the "King" (of rock and roll), so he can symbolically represent God being "the King." Elvis was also dressed in white, which often represents righteousness.

One time I simply had a dream with lyrics in it that I knew from the radio. The lyrics playing in the dream were, "Feel the rain on your skin, no one else can feel it for you, only you can let it in." I remember hearing it on the radio, but I had no clue who sang it or what the title of the song was. I was in the middle of planning to go away for a week to focus on my writing, when I asked my son to look up the title to the song I heard in my dream. I gave him a few of the lyrics and kind of sang it for him, and he quickly found it—"Unwritten" by Natasha Bedingfield. While my son was looking up the title, I was sharing with someone that I felt God was telling me to focus on writing my book! My book was "unwritten" and the song title was "Unwritten." The lyrics were profound and went on to encourage me that only I could write about my experience. Guess what one of the lines in the song was as I was actually planning my trip at that very moment to go away and write—"Today is where your book begins." This life with God is an incredibly fun adventure if you allow yourself to be open to how He may be speaking to you all the time! (Check out the lyrics at: http://www.songlyrics.com/natasha-bedingfield/unwritten-lyrics/.)

## JEDI DREAM TIPS FOR INTERPRETING MUSIC

- Consider the name of the artist. Tom Petty, for instance, may have to do with being or acting petty (mean).

- See if the title of the song itself has significance, like the examples "How Great Thou Art" and "Unwritten."

- Perhaps the chorus repeats an important thought or idea to ponder.

- What type of song is it? Upbeat, sad, etc. This may reveal more information for interpretation, such as your emotions.

- What genre of music is it? Country, pop, heavy metal, contemporary Christian, etc. This can also be interpreted further.

- Do you like the song; does it have specific significance to you? If so, that may be what it's about.

- Do the lyrics answer a question you have or reflect the way you feel? An example could be if things are clearing up in your life, you may get a song like, "I Can See Clearly Now the Rain Is Gone," or "I'm Walking on Sunshine," etc.

- It can also have to do with musical terms and wordplays:

  - *Treble* can mean trouble.

  - *Fret* can mean worry, etc.

  - *Note* may indicate to take note or take notes.

- Consider other musical terms such as *harmony, symphony, tone, notes*, etc.

## Musical Instruments

Instruments usually represent a person or the function or attributes of the specific instrument. There are thousands of interpretations for this category, because not only are there instruments but each instrument has numerous parts and names, and many times this is the focus instead of the instrument overall. For instance, is it a guitar in the dream that is important or is the focus the fret? If so, perhaps it has to do with worrying or *fretting*. Is it in tune? If not, perhaps it indicates that something needs to be fine-tuned. Is the focus that it's hollow? If so, do you feel lonely? Is a chord being played? This may reveal that several people need to come into one accord (a chord) in order to be more successful (sound better).

Let's look at a few other examples of instruments:

- *Percussion instruments* usually keep the beat or rhythm, so they often represent setting the pace or leading others. The surface of a percussion instrument resonates, so it may also indicate saying something that really "resonates" with others (makes sense). Pay attention to wordplays in this category, too, such as a snare drum may be a caution not to get en*snared* (be involved) in something.

- *Bowed string instruments* usually have to do with humility and heart strings or emotions. I have found the harp usually represents God's heart strings. A cello usually represents sadness or humility because of the deep or low sound. "Low" usually represents humility or sadness. The word *bowed* also represents humility, as in bowed before the king.

- Is it a *woodwind instrument?* Wind is usually representative of the Holy Spirit. In the correct context, it may also represent someone who is just "full of air," which means what they're saying has little substance. Woodwinds also operate with keys, perhaps giving further insight or important "keys" to unlock understanding about something.

- *Brass instruments* may either have to do with being a spokesperson or "mouthpiece" and can be positive or negative. Angels are mentioned in Scripture as blowing the trumpet. Also look up the meaning for *brass*.

- *Guitars* were already mentioned, but generally speaking it has to do with heart strings or emotions.

- *Keyboards or piano* have many interesting meanings in dreams, such as learning "lessons" or "keys" to understanding something. The sustain pedal may be a hidden indication to "press in" and wait. Maybe it even reveals that a loan or house note will be held out for a long time. The type or brand of instrument may be part of the interpretation, as well. A grand piano may reveal something grand or a big deal.

Consider the specific instrument, and as always, check the Bible first because there are many references to instruments. Cymbals, for example, represent someone who speaks without love. First Corinthians 13:1 says, *"Though I speak with the tongues of men and of angels, but have not love, I have become sounding brass or a clanging cymbal."* *Cymbal* may also be a hidden wordplay for a *symbol*.

## NATURE AND NATURAL ELEMENTS

Nature and natural elements in a dream are simply trees, rocks, water, fire, stars, clouds and rain, etc. They can also be gemstones, wood, storms, earthquakes, tornadoes, etc. The primary way to interpret this category is simply by the attributes and function of the symbol. There are tons of these elements in the Bible, so as a constant reminder, always check ancient Scripture first! Let's take a look at a few examples.

- *Rock*: A rock is a hard substance, so in the positive it may represent things like strength or stability. In the negative, it may indicate something "hard" or difficult. It can also represent someone's heart being hard or unresponsive emotionally.

- *Palm tree*: A palm tree grows upright. *Upright* refers to the heart being upright (see Jeremiah 10:5). It may also represent someone who worships Jesus; palm branches were used to worship Him as they cried out, *"Hosanna! Blessed is He who comes in the name of the Lord! The King of Israel!"* as He entered the city (John 12:13).

- *Vapor*: A vapor disappears quickly, therefore it usually represents something that is temporary. In Scripture it can represent life, which is here today and gone tomorrow (see James 4:14).

The primary way to interpret this category is to simply consider the attributes and function of the symbol. Attributes are usually the description of a symbol. Consider its shape, surface, placement, size, etc. Pay attention if it is smooth, rough, big, small, etc. These descriptions will help you when you think of what else in your life is going "smoothly," what things are "rough" or difficult, big or small, etc.

As with many other categories to interpret, always consider if a symbol could somehow represent a person. The best way to do that is to ask yourself how a person could be like a specific symbol or object. More insight on how to do this is in the "Objects and Elements" section below.

## NUMBERS

*Numbers* is a very difficult category to interpret. One of the main things I want to express about this category is to make sure you use the ancient Hebraic numbering system, which is called the *gematria*. In Hebrew, there are technically no numbers. Instead, there are letters that have a numeric value. This makes the meaning so much deeper when numbers are involved because their letters are also pictures that tell a whole story in and of themselves.

If we're not careful to use the Hebraic numbering system called the *gematria*, it's easy to slip into some very dangerous occult numbering systems called numerology. Numerology is a type of fortune-telling and it is an abomination to God, which means He hates it with passion. It's a form of witchcraft. If you have delved into numerology, tarot cards, etc., I plead with you to tell God you're sorry and then never do it again. It's important to even use the words, "I renounce it," which means to put it away from you and never do it again. It means you no longer want to come into agreement with it anymore. We often get involved in these types of things very innocently, but the Bible says that God's people perish for lack of knowledge. Now that you know, you are held account-able to God, and I again encourage you to repent and renounce these things if you've been involved in them.

Throughout ancient Scripture there are extensive patterns asso-ciated with numbers. You can download our *Dreamscapes® Dream Dictionary* app for both Apple and Android devices to access the research we've done for numbers found in Scripture.

## OBJECTS AND ELEMENTS

Objects and elements, or basic symbols in dreams, are the most fun to interpret. The thing you must always keep in mind within any category is that sometimes it's not about the thing you're inter-preting as much as it is about the condition of it, the things that surround the object, what's being done with it, how it's being used, what your thoughts are about it are, etc.

To begin interpreting a symbol, consider what its purpose is, what its condition is, what it's being used for, if it's being used cor-rectly, the size, the color, etc. All of these things are important for a correct interpretation.

I have often found that unique symbols in dreams usually rep-resent facets of people. It's as if the dream is saying, "You are like this object." Watch carefully how you describe a symbol and see if it could also be describing someone's character, like "rough around the edges," etc.

## PEOPLE, CAREERS, CHARACTERS

People are among the most difficult categories to interpret because there are so many factors to consider. In Scripture people were literal, but they were also used as shadows and types representing many things such as disobedience, nations, etc. People are *most often* representative of aspects of the *dreamer*. Always consider this *first* before applying it to other things or people. I've explained in this section many different ways to approach interpreting people, but to quickly give you an overview, here are some insights to take into consideration:

- People may represent their attitudes and actions in the dream.

- They may represent an aspect of the dreamer, such as a similar attitude, a similar life or situation, etc.

- They may represent what they do for a living. For instance, a financial advisor may represent financial advice or money.

- Their age may reveal a level of maturity or immaturity.

- They may represent the nation they are from if that is what is most obvious about them.

- Actors may represent things about integrity or "character."

- They may represent their symbolic role in a family or in the dreamer's life, such as father, mother, son, sister, etc.

- People can represent issues or situations you're dealing with.

- They may represent what the meaning of their name is and the Scripture that goes with the name.

- They may be spiritual beings, even angels! (See Hebrews 13:2).

- Their size may reveal things like how big an issue is, a maturity level, etc.

- Their age may reveal how long an issue has been going on, a maturity level, or the number may be symbolic.

- The description of their body will reveal many things. For instance, are they skinny, fat, a dwarf or small person, short, disabled, etc.?

- Famous people can be symbolic for the roles they've played, movies they've been in, or a wordplay on their name. ("Tom Cruise" may reveal either that something is about to take off—*cruise*—or perhaps it reminds the dreamer of the movie *Risky Business* and it's a warning about business decisions.) Remember to take into consideration *your* opinion of them.

- People may be literal depending on life circumstances, if the dreamer is a prayer intercessor, the influence the dreamer has in their life, etc.

- While people may be literal, they are *most often* symbolic and most often about the dreamer!

- The person in your dream you know is there, but you never see his face is the Holy Spirit (if positive!).

- Angels and demons are literally angels and demons.

- Cartoon people usually represent "character" or integrity. They may also represent what they are known for. For instance, Road Runner may represent being swift or smart.

- Familiar people may represent things you're *familiar* with or they may reveal *familiar* spirits that are in your family.

- They may be types and shadows of things to come.

Something else to make you aware of, which God revealed to me years ago, is that you usually are not to share dreams you feel are about other people with them unless He specifically tells you. Most dreams are about facets of the dreamer, but when it is about someone else, the instruction is to simply pray for them unless you're told otherwise.

One other note to remember is that dreams can have multiple meanings all at the same time, so when there are people in your dreams, I encourage you to look at it symbolically first, but always cover your bases with prayer for people just in case it's literal.

### The Descriptions of People

You will begin to find with interpreting your dreams that the descriptions and unspoken observations are sometimes more important than the actual symbol itself. It's certainly true of interpreting people, too.

The interpretation of the people in your dreams may have more to do with what they look like, how they act, the description of what they are wearing, or what they're doing. For instance, it's important to pay attention to their age, size, body description, what clothes they are wearing, and anything that stands out or is an exception, such as if the person is a dwarf, handicapped, fat, skinny, muscular, etc.

The descriptions you uncover may also end up describing something specific in your life such as a job, a relationship, an issue, or a situation. If a person is disabled or a dwarf, ask yourself if you feel disabled anywhere in your life or stunted in your growth, perhaps on the job, in a relationship, etc.

## Acquaintances

Acquaintances are people you know, but not well. This is a tricky category because you have to be careful to rule everything else out first. As mentioned previously, several years ago a lady called me about a dream she had. She was disturbed because she saw a man die in her dream. We reviewed the dream and I asked her if he had any symbolic reference for her. She said no, he was just an acquaintance from high school. We brainstormed about what he may represent. We even looked up the meaning of his name, but it just didn't seem to fit.

I had been taught that when someone dies in a dream it usually means the end of something, which can be true, or it may mean dying to your carnal nature and being raised up spiritually—and that dying in dreams was always a good thing. So as a last resort after brainstorming with her, I simply told her what I was taught—that dying in dreams is good and it means the person is probably dying to an area of his selfish nature and starting to be led by the Spirit. I cautioned her to pray for him just in case her dream was literal, and she did.

Days later she called again and asked me if I remembered her dream. I answered yes, and she went on to tell me that the man actually died three days after her dream. I was relieved we had discussed praying for him, but I felt horrible that I relayed what I was taught regarding death in dreams and that it's not literal.

That night I received a dream from the Lord. In the dream, He told me that when acquaintances are in your dreams and they have no other symbolic reference for you, the dreams are literal and

He wants us to pray for them because there's no one else in their life praying for them right now. The context will reveal what to pray about.

One lesson to learn from my experience is that not only do you need to ask a lot of questions when interpreting your dreams, but if you are helping other people interpret their dreams you also need to get to know the dreamer and how they typically dream. This dreamer often gets literal things, which is rare. Her prayer wasn't meant to prevent him from dying necessarily, but to pray that he would be prepared to die and to pray for his family. This dreamer has a calling from God to pray for difficult things for people; I didn't know that at the time, and I neglected to ask questions about her typical dream life. Please learn from my mistake!

### Angels and Demons in Dreams and Life

The word *angel* means "messenger." Whenever you have dreams, visions, or real-life experiences with angels, they are there to give you a message. Everything about them is sending a message to you! Pay attention to their clothing, their expression, the color of their hair and eyes, the condition or description of their clothing or hair, what they are doing or not doing, their size, and anything else about them. Absolutely everything about them will give you deeper insight into the message they are there to deliver.

Demons are usually called by their personality, actions, etc., such as fear, shame, guilt, etc. If they have horns, that speaks of the authority they carry because horns represent authority. There are different levels of authority for all spiritual beings.

### Careers

Careers are metaphors for things they represent and their role or function. The following are some examples:

- A doctor or nurse may represent healing or a need for healing in an area of your life, such as emotionally, spiritually, financially, relationally, physically, etc.

- Teachers may represent either giving or receiving instruction, etc.

- Judges may have to do with judging a person or situation, being judged, or that God is the only Judge.

- A police officer may represent protection, justice, or perhaps someone who is legalistic.

- A dentist may reveal issues that need to be straightened out in relationships, because teeth most often represent relationships with people and dentists or orthodontists straighten teeth or fix the issue that is causing pain.

## Cartoon Characters

I had an incredible dream once in which I dissolved into a cartoon character. It was an amazing experience! God revealed to me it represented my *character* was changing (for the good!). Specific cartoon characters will have specific insights. Two quick examples are Mickey Mouse and Snoopy. Mickey Mouse has big ears, so he usually represents listening (with the intent to respond and not just hear). Snoopy has a big nose and noses usually represent discernment (insight or understanding). He may also represent someone who likes to snoop, too. Snoopy is personally my favorite cartoon character, and I love how he giggles, so for me he would also represent fun!

## Dead People

Let's clarify a few things concerning this category. First, you have people in your dreams who in real life are dead, but in your dream they are alive. Many times when this happens it's usually symbolic of an area in your life, such as a job, relationship, skill or talent you have, etc., that was symbolically dead but now has returned. Years ago a dear friend of mine died. Only days after her funeral, I began to have dreams about her coming onto a train I was on. I would wake up devastated because the pain was still so fresh; I couldn't understand why she was in my dreams that way. It took me several weeks, but I eventually discovered she was symbolic, representing my writing that I had recently allowed to stop, or "die." The train represented "training" others and that I needed to bring my writing back to life, just as she had come back to life in the dream, so I could write training manuals for dream classes.

Then there are dreams where people in your real life are alive in reality, but dead in your dream. This can be difficult to sort through, but most of the time, the first thing to consider is whatever the person symbolically represents for you. This is usually representative of an area in your life (the symbolic representation will reveal what) that once was active and alive, but has ended.

Dead people can often represent a dead issue that needs to be buried or forgiven so you can move on. Death in dreams often represents the end of something, such as a relationship, job, an issue, etc. Keep in mind that literal elements are always possible in dreams, so I'm careful to remind people above all else to pray.

There are also amazing dreams that allow us to see loved ones who have died. As always, I recommend looking at the symbolic representation first with dreams, but there are some I consider to be actual spiritual encounters. Sometimes someone we love will die and we are concerned with unresolved issues or if they had eternal salvation. I've encountered dozens, if not hundreds of dreams where it was as though the actual person was allowed by God to come to us in a dream and let us know things are okay. Don't freak out on me! God is God and we are not. God can choose to do anything He wants. Whether those dreams are the actual spirit of the person God allowed to come to us in a dream or God creating a dream to encourage us in a way we needed to be encouraged, we won't know this side of Heaven. Either way, it's an awesome experience to be given peace and emotional healing through a dream!

You may be saying to yourself, "It's biblically inaccurate to speak to the dead." I get that objection a lot. First, let me clarify that we do not know if it's actually the person or God creating a dream of the person to simply encourage us. We also can't know for sure if we have caused ourselves to dream a dream like this, but most people I speak with concerning this issue say it was much more lucid and felt more like a spiritual experience than a dream. Second, ancient Scripture says that God is not God of the dead but of the living. Those who have eternal salvation are alive in Christ. Many will use the example of Saul in the Old Testament to prove it's wrong, but I would argue that in the time of the Old Testament, Christ Jesus had not been crucified yet or brought back to life, and therefore, people prior to the crucifixion were not yet raised to life.

Last, I would caution you that we are not to seek speaking to those who have died; however, God can author anything He desires. My instruction would be to not pursue it, but simply pray and ask the Lord to reveal the answers you're looking for and allow God to do it how He sees is most beneficial and fitting.

## "Familiar" People

When someone seems familiar to you while you are in the dream but you don't specifically know who they are, it may be an indication you are dealing with an issue that is provoked by *familiar* spirits. Familiar spirits are demons that study your family and try to torment each generation with the same issues, such as drugs, alcohol, fear, etc. A clue that this is what you're encountering in your dream is that the word "familiar" keeps coming to mind and there are no other interpretation ideas for them. On another note, familiar people may be symbolic for situations, issues, or things you are *familiar* with. Remember, people are very symbolic in dreams for other things.

## Family Members

### Fathers

Years ago, I had a dream about a father and I heard the Holy Spirit say, *"Fathers in dreams are usually there to teach you something, because fathers are supposed to teach."* Pay attention to what the father is doing or saying or not doing or not saying. It may be positive or negative. If it's negative, it may be how you're acting: if it's positive, it may be how you need to act or it may be encouraging you to see that you're on the right track. Pay attention to facial expressions, actions, moods, clothing, etc.

Fathers may reveal a spiritual blessing, too, because it is the father in the Hebrew culture who blesses his children.

Fathers in dreams may also reveal father issues you may be struggling with in real life. Because most of our dreams are emotional processing, it's common to process ongoing issues we have a hard time dealing with. On the other hand, if your father in real life is a positive symbol for you, sometimes a father in a dream may also represent Father God. Make sure the context is correct and in keeping with the loving nature of God.

### Mothers

Mothers can be tricky to interpret; however, I have personally found they often represent either the church or things like attitudes, habits, responses, or reactions that you learned from your mother growing up. Mothers also nurture, so sometimes they can be an example of how to nurture someone or something specifically or how you yourself might need to be nurtured. Of course, mothers may also reveal mother issues if you struggle with your relationship with her.

## Children

Children may represent childlike faith or a level of maturity. Pay attention to their age. While a mother can and does dream of her literal child, I have personally found that children most often represent the dreamer's spiritual gifts and abilities. The reason is because Scripture says children are a gift from God. In dreams, if children represent your spiritual gifting, they will align with the order that the children were born in. In other words, your oldest child will represent the spiritual gift you first discovered, etc.

## Sisters and Brothers

Sisters and brothers are usually metaphors for those who have chosen Jesus Christ as their Lord and Savior. Scripture considers believers in Jesus Christ to be *brothers and sisters in Christ*. There is always the chance it may literally be about your siblings or it may also reveal an aspect of you that is similar to them.

## Grandparents

Grandparents usually represent generations and spiritual inheritances, especially if it's a grandmother. Grandpa may be teaching you about your inheritance. Grandfathers may indicate a spiritual blessing. Grandfather may also be a wordplay for grandfather clause, which can mean to provide provision that exempts people from newly created laws, etc.

## Aunts, Uncles, Cousins

I have found that relatives usually reveal things that are "related" to *you!* Other considerations are what your opinion of them is, what you think of when you think of them, if they were good at something, if they had a bad habit, etc.

## Spouses

Sometimes spouses represent Jesus if you are a Christian believer because He is the Groom to the Bride of Christ. While every person in a dream can be interpreted literally, it's rare unless that is how you typically dream. It took me between three and four years to figure out what my husband at the time meant in my dreams. Simply by process of elimination through hundreds of dreams, I discovered my husband for me represented me and my gift of teaching. Why would a spouse represent us? Because when married, the two become *one* in the sight of God, so your spouse is literally "part of you." Marriage is also about commitment, so your spouse can represent something you're committed to, just as my husband at the time represented teaching for me. I was committed to teaching about dreams.

### Your First Love and Former Relationships

The person you were first in love with often represents Jesus, because He is mentioned in Scripture as our first love (see Rev. 2:4). Make sure the context is positive and correct for this interpretation.

This is probably one of the most common dreams people have. It's a really disturbing feeling, especially if you're happily with someone else, to have dreams that you're back with an old love. With the exception of your First Love, Jesus, former relationships usually represent old ways, habits, addictions, thoughts, issues, etc. coming back into your life. Remember, people are usually archetypes for abstract things.

### Famous People

Famous people usually represent the role they play, something you think of when you think of them, their reputation, your opinion of them, or a wordplay for their character or their real name. There are thousands of examples, but just to help you brainstorm, here a few examples:

#### Oprah Winfrey

She usually represents having a major influence with others with what you have to say, because she had a "talk" show and she has major influence.

### Tom Cruise

He may be a wordplay for something that will take off, or "cruise," such as a business, etc. Speaking of business, he may also represent the movie *Risky Business* and may alert you to business decisions.

### Justin Bieber

I recently had him in one of my dreams and it took me a while to figure out. He had just experienced a downfall because of his choices in real life, so I wondered if that's what he represented metaphorically. Weeks later, I was flipping through Netflix to find a movie to watch and saw his movie *Believe,* and suddenly realized that's what he meant in the context of my dream. I reluctantly had my picture taken with him in the dream, and after I interpreted it as a result of the movie, I realized the dream was showing me that although I was reluctant, I was beginning to "get the picture" and embrace faith and *believe* God for something in a specific area of my life.

### Huey Lewis and the News

They may reveal a piece of news or information that has or will come to pass. They may also represent something related to "The Power of Love," which is one of their songs.

## Known but Unknown People

These are people you know in your dream but don't really exist in real life. Most of the time I have found these people to represent the dreamer, though not always. I have met dreamers who have dreamed of people they didn't know at the time, but later actually met them in real life! A good rule of thumb is to always apply the interpretation of the person to yourself first, then consider other possibilities.

## Names and Their Meaning

When you have people in your dream and they don't have an obvious symbolic reference for you, it may be that the meaning of their name that is the key to the interpretation. I recommend *The Name Book: Over 10,000 Names, Their Meanings, Origins, and Spiritual Significance* by Dorothy Astoria because it not only gives you the meaning of the name, but it also gives the spiritual connotation and a Scripture with each name. I have found that the associated Scripture has been the answer to the interpretation of many of my dreams, sometimes even more important than the meaning of their name, although both are usually incredibly helpful!

Although it doesn't hurt to look up the meaning for every name in all your dreams, I see many people who reference the meaning of a name first, when in reality I have found it to be something to do when all else doesn't seem to fit. As with anything in dream interpretation, stay balanced and stay open to all possibilities. It's important to stay on the interpretation road and not drive off into a ditch on either side.

## Nationalities

Whenever you have people in your dream who have specific nationalities that stand out, the first thing to do is consider what the country represents. For instance, whenever I have people from India in my dream who don't exist in real life, it usually represents that I am in an area of unbelief in my life. As previously mentioned, the reason India represents unbelief is because they serve millions of gods in India and not the one true God. This is not to say there aren't Christians there, because there absolutely are!

Another thing people or clothing from other countries may indicate is that you may have a call from God to that country. If this is the case, you will receive many other confirmations. As always, never make major decisions based on dreams without God confirming it in His Word and through many other avenues.

Remember, the Bible says our own heart can deceive us and we can dream things we want to dream, so we have to respond with caution.

## The Invisible Man

Have you ever had someone in your dream and knew they were there but never saw their face? If the context is in keeping with God's nature, this invisible man, usually portrayed as your friend, is usually God's Holy Spirit! The reason you don't see Him is because you don't see spirit—the Spirit is the invisible realm. The exciting thing about the invisible realm is that ancient Scripture reveals it is more real than the visible one!

## Sexual

This is a category no one likes to talk about but everyone wants to know the meaning of so they can gain some peace! This category is about sexual encounters and not about things like kissing or holding hands or hugging. Those will have a different interpretation and fall under the category of "Actions and Situations."

I continually hear people teach that sexual types of dreams should simply be disregarded because they are from the enemy, or they teach sex dreams are to be "flushed," disposed of, forgotten. I couldn't disagree more strongly! These dreams are usually warning dreams, and they are usually trying to get your attention and save you from making horrible choices.

The place to begin interpreting this category is to begin by first understanding what God says about sex. God's viewpoint about sex is that it should take place only inside of marriage between one woman and one man. Anything else outside of these parameters is ungodly and must be interpreted that way also within dreams. Having homosexual encounters in dreams, for instance, usually represents being *intimately involved* with others who are just like you (same sex) and are telling you what you want to hear, and these dreams are always warning dreams because God created us to be with the opposite sex.

If your dream is about having sex with your actual spouse of the opposite sex, then the dream is probably very positively interpreted unless the dream was negative. Remember, context is everything! Beautiful marital sex reveals intimacy, either emotionally with your spouse or it may also reveal beautiful intimacy with God. Why? Because Jesus is considered the husband of the Bride of Christ, and believers will one day marry or become fully committed to Him—He will become our metaphorical spouse.

The first thing to remember is that dreams are symbolic and sexual dreams don't mean what you probably think they mean. Most people will be shocked, but there are many examples in Scripture. For instance, God speaks of idolatry, which means to put something else before God, and compares those in it to harlots and adulterers. The reason is because it represents putting priority on something or someone other than God, and sometimes it involves money.

Symbolically, sex represents being incredibly intimate. Also keep in mind that different body parts have different meanings. Pay attention to what is happening within the dream, and this will help you to focus on what the main issue is. Typically, sex in dreams reveals getting *too involved* or intimate with something or someone. It can represent gossip, slander, or sharing information you probably shouldn't be sharing. The person you're having sex with in the dream, especially if it is not your spouse of the opposite sex, may represent issues, habits, addictions, or anything you might be too involved in, even something such as work, etc.

Let me give you an example of a dream most others would tell you to throw away or "flush." One time a lady asked me about a dream she had where she was doing sexual things to her son's private parts. She was incredibly disturbed by it, as anyone would typically be. The interpretation was that she was getting too "involved" with giving him advice that pertained to his "private" matters in his relationship with his wife. She was telling him what he wanted to hear so she would "please" him instead of telling him what he needed to hear. Do you see how a sexual dream could represent being involved in private things, and that pleasing someone sexually may refer to pleasing them in real life or telling them what they wanted to hear? In real life a mother should not be intimate with a son, so this was a warning dream that what she was doing was wrong. It got her attention, she knew exactly what it was about, and she repented.

One time I asked God why some dreams were so disgusting or violent, and He revealed to me that's how it actually is in the spirit realm. He wants us to see how disgusting some things we do really are. In Scripture, God often told disobedient people they were like harlots because He wanted to convey to them how hurtful and unfaithful they were being. He gave them an example they could relate to.

With all that said, there is a chance you were in a wrong environment where disgusting things have happened and you received the spiritual residue from it. The way to know is to interpret it and see if it fits for you personally with anything going on in your life or if it pertains to the people in the dream. If not, I would discard it and ask God to get your attention another way if it's something you were supposed to pay attention to. If you have a heart to want to understand and obey, God is gracious and faithful to help you figure it out. He doesn't just give us one chance and we're in trouble—He is ever patient and quick to forgive a truly repentant heart. There is *nothing* He won't forgive if you mean it! It truly is that easy.

## TRANSPORTATION

There are hundreds of types of transportation, from boats, cars, and vehicles, to planes, hot air balloons, trains, and more. Transportation in dreams represents that which gets us from one place in life to another. Transportation can be symbolic for things we're involved in—jobs, ministries, relationships, motives, etc.

Take note of the size and condition of the transportation. Is it a bicycle that requires more effort and involves only you, or is it a jumbo jet that involves hundreds of people? This helps reveal what it's referring to in your life.

Pay attention to the type of transportation and the characteristics of it. Note the specific type and brand. If it's a car, look at the color, what make and model it is, etc. For example, if you are driving a Dodge, perhaps you are able to "dodge" the things that would hinder your progress, or maybe you're "dodging" responsibility. If it's a boat, is it a tugboat, speedboat, dingy, or the Titanic? If you're riding on the Titanic, it could be warning you what you're involved in (a company, ministry, etc.) will not succeed and you need to "jump ship." If it's an ambulance, perhaps God is bringing you to a place of healing emotionally, spiritually, or physically. If you are driving the ambulance, it may reveal you are helping others get to a place of emotional, spiritual, or physical healing—perhaps you are counseling a friend, etc.

Notice where you are in the vehicle, which may reveal your role. Are you driving and making the decisions? Should you be? Maybe it's about your marriage, and your husband should be the one driving and he's not. Are you in the backseat? Maybe that says you are part of someone else's company, ministry, etc., or maybe it's a wordplay indicating that you are "taking a backseat" and not being as involved as others are or as involved as you should be. On the other hand, maybe you're supposed to be in the backseat and not driving or making the decisions. Also consider if you are being a "backseat driver" (someone who likes to call the shots).

If you're on a plane, are you part of a big company or does it mean you have the ability to fly high above your circumstances? God once revealed to me inside a dream that a plane can sometimes be a wordplay indicating God is making something "plain" or obvious to you. Keep asking why one particular type of transportation is being used versus another.

## IDIOMS, RIDDLES, WORDPLAYS

### Idioms

I think one of the most creative and fun ways God speaks in dreams is through the use of idioms. Idioms are sayings or expressions that don't necessarily have meaning, and it's rare they are grammatically correct on their own, such as "bend over backward," "keeping tabs," or "he's a wet blanket." It is slang or jargon that simply has an understanding of its own. *Idiom* comes from the Greek word *idiousthai,* meaning "to make one's own," from *idios,* "own, personal, private." So you could almost say that God makes His own personal, private language that is hidden in treasures we call dreams!

**God makes His own personal, private language that is hidden in treasures we call dreams!**

One of the first idioms I remember when I began to record my dreams was a sentence written in huge letters on the wall of my master bedroom. It was encouragement to me and direction from God that the answer was obvious—"The writing was on the wall." Another time I remember someone in a dream having a "hard time swallowing something," as in having a hard time believing something. I find idioms in my dreams every week it seems. I look for the action in the dream, or the verb, and begin to see if it fits into a well-known saying or an idiom.

One of the funniest ones I remember discovering (and it might be one of those that "you had to be there" for it to be funny, so please forgive me in advance for what might seem like an exaggeration or no big deal) was in a dream where I had seen one of the pedals to a piano and I took it from the top of a chest of drawers and put in down on the floor on top of some papers. I know nothing about pianos, so I researched to see what that pedal was called, and it was the damper pedal. I then began to laugh as I discovered God was showing me that I had "gotten something off my chest" (chest of drawers) but in doing so I "put a damper on things"! I could not stop laughing; not because I had been so insensitive and ruined an opportunity to shine the light of God into a situation, but because I was amazed God would hide these incredibly creative treasures in our dreams.

I often feel like I am playing charades with God in my dreams and I'm trying to guess what He's trying to tell me. It's as if He's saying, "It sounds like...two syllables..." when He uses homophones, idioms, wordplays, etc. There are hundreds and hundreds of idioms; there are numerous websites with lists of them. You can then do a specific search for an item or object. For instance, if there is a duck in your dream, or any other thing or animal, simply do a search with one specific word and it will show you the idioms it has listed that include that word. You'll often find there will be an idiom or phrase that perfectly fits the action or focus of the dream. Idioms are also listed at the bottom of dictionary meanings, too.

Another thing to look for in dreams are hidden parts of words. Sometimes a word can "come apart" if you will, and it can mean other things or perhaps more than one thing. One time someone said she saw a blood blister that was "see-through" in a dream. The first word that came to my mind instead of "see-through" was *transparent* or *apparent*. I believe the Holy Spirit revealed to me that it meant all three—see-through, as in this was an issue that the dreamer was able to discern, or "see through," and it possibly meant to "see something through" to the end until it was complete. The symbol also meant that this was a bloodline issue (blood blister) that had to do with "a parent"—get it? *Apparent* meant "a parent." This was an issue that was "below the surface" (of the skin) that had to do with one of the dreamer's parents, and it was "festering" or causing pain (the blister). The word *transparent* also came into play; *trans* can mean something that is conveyed from one person to another or through an impression. Again, this had to do with something that "a parent" was conveying to the dreamer that was causing things to fester. *Fester* could also represent bitterness. I checked with the dreamer and all of these interpretations, to use an idiom, "hit the nail on the head!" They were completely accurate!

Sometimes the wordplay is in the way a word is used or in the way you reword a phrase, object, etc. There was one dream I had where someone was taking something apart. That someone in my dream represented God, and He was saying that if things didn't work properly or go as He instructed others (and possibly myself, I'm sure), He could dismantle things—remove the mantle. In the dream, the word *dismantle* was not used. However, when I went to write the dream down, it's ironic I chose that specific word to best describe what was going on. That frequently happens for me. As I am writing something down, the words I end up using are actually the interpretation.

I have found hidden wordplays within words as well. I once interpreted a dream scene where someone was in a river and the person found that the pull of the water was strong and couldn't get out. Normally, we look at a river as a move of God. However, in this instance, it was simply a wordplay meaning the person dreaming was "getting caught up" (involved) in something that was *currently* going on. The wordplay here was with the strong current in the river. The word *current* stood out to me and I knew it meant something that was current, or in progress now. It might even have to do with money— "currency." See how deep you can continue to go into interpretation?

It usually means several things, not one or the other, but all or many. I brainstorm and come up with as many things as possible. Usually, there will be a running theme and things will begin to naturally fit, especially with the rest of the dream context.

Another way God uses wordplays is with existing terms or words, but with a different context. For instance, take the sport of football. If you have football in a dream, it can mean many things. It could represent that something needs to be "tackled" (confronted, solved, etc.), that people are "receiving" what you are "passing" on to them (teaching, advice, etc.), that you need to wear the "helmet" of salvation (having the mind of Christ), that you are protected (padding), or maybe that others are "opposing" you (opposing team). You can then look at the numbers used in scoring in football. It's ironic that football scores often will have the numbers 3 and 7 in them—God's numbers!

I was interpreting dreams for people inside of a dream once, and I said to them (by what I believe was God showing me an insight) that one key word will open up the meaning to the whole interpretation. Hence, my fascination with words! Hopefully these examples will provoke your thinking and cause you to look at words in a whole new way!

### Riddles—Keys to Your Destiny

The first example of a riddle I had to figure out in one of my dreams took me two years to solve. I was told I would write a book in the dream. There were a lot of details to the dream, but the major details were that my book was being compared to someone else's teaching on the same subject. In the dream their teaching was a book (in real life, it was an audio recording) and my book was to the right of it with the same exact cover (different colors, though), but our titles were slightly different—and *that* was the riddle that took me two years to resolve. The other title was *Passage to Intimacy* and my title was *Intimate Passage.* After two very long years of wondering why the subtle difference, the

Lord showed me that it contained the *key* to helping people *reach their destinies!*

Here is what God revealed to me: first, He showed me the two books in my dream with the *Passage to Intimacy* one on the left and mine, titled *Intimate Passage,* on the right.

| Passage to Intimacy | Intimate Passage |
|---|---|

He asked me, "What is the main difference in the titles?" I looked and looked, and finally had an epiphany and said out loud, "In my book title, *intimacy comes first!*" And *that* was the hidden key to share with others—including you—about how to reach your destiny! This is the book that was in the dream! It's my sincere prayer it will help you reach your spiritual destiny as you discover becoming intimate with God is the first and most important key to reaching your spiritual destiny in God.

When you put intimacy with God first, the passage to your destiny automatically pursues *you.* In other words, *do not pursue destiny! Pursue God and destiny will overtake you!* You won't have to try. Your destiny comes out of your intimate relationship with God. There is no higher priority in life than to be intimate with God—to become, by faith, His child, His servant, His co-laborer, and ultimately, His friend. Moses was considered a friend of God, Enoch walked with God, and Jesus speaks over and over about what it means to be a friend. A friend is someone you can count on, who would lay down his or her life for you. Jesus is your Friend and He paid the ultimate price when He laid down His life for you. He is the Friend who sticks closer than a brother, and He is faithful in all things. If you want to know more about how to become a friend of Jesus, and ultimately God the Father, read Chapter 10, The Secret Gateway: Invite the Light.

Since that dream, I find that about 30-50 percent of my personal dreams contain riddles, idioms, or homonyms to solve in order to figure out the meaning. Riddles are all through the Bible. We discuss these in more depth in our courses, workshops, and seminars.

## Wordplays

One of the strongest ways God speaks to me in dreams is through wordplays. As I began to think about how to write about wordplays, however, it became confusing because I was finding I categorize a lot of things as wordplays and I wasn't sure if I could distinguish each of them.

What is a wordplay? Simply put, it's a play on words. It's a word or group of words that can have an alternate meaning.

One way wordplays can happen is when a word or group of words that are being used mimic or sound like another word. For example, a porpoise may really mean *purpose* or destiny.

The first time I remember God using a wordplay in a dream of mine was in a dream where I was observing Patty Duke in an empty room smiling (if you are too young to know who she is, she had a television show and has been in several movies since). The odd thing was, in my dream she was Caucasian but had an Afro hairdo. I remember in the dream staring at her and saying, "Patty Duke?! Why Patty Duke?" Over and over I repeated, "Patty Duke? Patty Duke?" Then I heard the Holy Spirit either say or give me the unction to say, "Put up your dukes." At that time in my life, I was coming out of what we affectionately call the "dark night of the soul"—desert time. I didn't know if I would make it through, and this dream was encouraging me to "put up my dukes" and fight my negative thinking. Thinking is sometimes represented by hair, and the Afro indicated that my thinking was "dark" and would eventually lead me down a course (*coarse*) that would be "rough" if I continued in that direction. At the time I was feeling empty, like the room in my dream, and meditating on wrongs that had been done to me instead of "smiling" like Patty Duke was and choosing joy. There were two wordplays in that dream. Patty Duke meant put up my dukes, and the description of the hair was coarse (rough), which revealed the course of thinking I was choosing.

Another time God used a friend of mine as a wordplay. Her name is Shirley Downing. It was a wordplay for "surely," meaning *certainly*, and "down" as in depression or difficult time. Another example that was revealed to me while I was inside the dream was Lego (the toy). The Holy Spirit told me it could mean "let go." One of my favorite wordplays is Sears, the store. I was shown it was a wordplay for *seers*, or those who "see" in the spirit. I told that to a seer friend of mine and she about flipped out because she was also a seer and her dad worked for Sears when she was growing up. The examples are endless. I would caution you not to go to extremes in this area, though. I have seen people stretch this so far that it simply wasn't even close or didn't make any sense.

The first thing I typically do when reading over a dream is look for words that could have other meanings. This is the most common way wordplays are used, and they're called homophones. A homophone is one of two or more words—such as *night* and *knight*, *profit* and *prophet*, etc.—that are pronounced the same but differ in meaning, origin, and sometimes spelling. An Internet search will reveal tons of sites with homonyms or homophones to give you hundreds of ideas.

## Examples

- Lego = let go
- Patty Duke = put up your dukes
- Porpoise = purpose
- Plane = plain

ENDNOTE

1. *BlueLetterBible*, s.v. "Fruit," G2590, accessed January 25, 2015, http://www.blueletterbible.org/lang/lexicon/lexicon.cfm?strongs=G2590.

# ABOUT TERESA WARD

TERESA WARD founded Above & Beyond in 2006. She has been a prolific dreamer since childhood – and still dreams all night, every night. Teresa studied dream interpretation for 4 years with a prominent international ministry that focuses on dream interpretation. While associated with them, she became a certified instructor and a certified dream interpreter. She has also participated with Dream Teams at various events such as conferences, festivals and the Super Bowl.

God often speaks to Teresa in her dreams, revealing how to interpret them and what things mean. She has personally documented and interpreted over 30,000 dreams and visions of her own, not to mention thousands for others between 2001 and 2014. She has discovered hidden keys and mysteries of how to interpret not only dreams and visions, but also numerous other experiences, circumstances, and events. God has released, commissioned and commanded her to share this revelation to help release others into their spiritual destiny.

Teresa has been appeared on TV, Blog Radio, at Seminars, Conferences, Workshops, Events, and Churches and offers spiritual acceleration courses, special events, and retreats dealing with the topics of dreams, encouraging women, intimacy with God, and marriage. She currently resides near Charleston, South Carolina, and has two amazing sons.

Above & Beyond was founded on the scripture found in Ephesians 3:14-21: For this reason I bow my knees to the Father of our Lord Jesus Christ, from whom the whole family in heaven and earth is named, that He would grant you, according to the riches of His glory, to be strengthened with might through His Spirit in the inner man, that Christ may dwell in your hearts through faith; that you, being rooted and grounded in love, may be able to comprehend with all the saints what is the width and length and depth and height—to know the love of Christ which passes knowledge; that you may be filled with all the fullness of God. Now to Him who is able to do exceedingly abundantly above [ABOVE & BEYOND!] all that we ask or think, according to the power that works in us, to Him be glory in the church by Christ Jesus to all generations, forever and ever. Amen.